Saddle, Sore

Saddle, Sore

RIDE HAPPY

RIDE COMFORTABLE

Molly Hurford

Saddle, Sore: Ride Comfortable, Ride Happy

Copyright © 2014 by Molly Hurford

Second Edition, 2016

More Information: saddlesorebook.com

To the rad women I've met since I discovered cycling.
You are all just the best.

A note to returning readers:

Writing this, I'm thinking about a talk I gave earlier this month. After I was done going through my spiel on making riding more comfortable, a woman came up to chat with me. "Before tonight, I thought being numb every ride was normal," she told me. And a week later, I got an email from her that a bike fit and saddle swap had made her go from numb to comfortable, and she was thrilled. It's a strange way to help people, but it's working. Too many women stop riding because of things like that, things that aren't talked about and can ruin a great sport for people.

When I first wrote the original edition of *Saddle, Sore*, I was amazed and overwhelmed at the support that the book had behind it. It came out two years ago, and I've given dozens of talks, sold thousands of copies, and answered hundreds of emails, all about our nether regions and the bike. Two years ago, I thought I'd maybe sell 100 books, if I was lucky. But it turns out I struck a nerve: people had questions, and they needed a place to go to find answers. It was a strange niche for someone to develop, but every time someone said that my book helped keep her riding, I felt an incredible sense of pride. Sure, it's not the sexiest topic. But it is an important one.

If you're a returning reader, you might be surprised to find a chapter in here for male riders. The original book was written for the growing female population of riders, but as I started giving talks at bike shops and answering a lot of questions for a lot of cyclists, I realized that it wasn't just women who were suffering in silence—there were plenty of male riders who were also having saddle sore issues, problems with numbness, and questions that they just couldn't ask their buddies. Because of that, this edition has some info for the men out there too—it's still largely about the ladies, but I wanted to make this book as accessible as possible to as many people as possible. You'll notice some new chapters on men's issues, but also some new ones for women, from questions relating to pregnancy and menopause, to issues that bigger riders face. And each section that was in the original *Saddle, Sore* has gotten an update as well: I've added new experts, answered more in-depth questions, and generally made some improvements with what I've learned over the years. And I'm hoping that it's even more helpful than the first edition.

So, enjoy, learn, and please share with the other cyclists in your life! And yes—I giggled every time I typed the word penis.

Love,
Molly

TABLE OF CONTENTS

INTRODUCTION

If you were on a ride and sprained your ankle, would you say something to the group you were riding with? Obviously, you wouldn't just suffer in silence. But what about when you're out on a ride, and you realize that you're cramping terribly because you're just about to get your period? Or you start feeling tingly, or numb, on the saddle? Most riders won't speak up. Most will suffer in silence, come home, and have no idea why they have massive saddle sores—if they even realize what a saddle sore looks like—or how to treat them.

Your level of experience doesn't matter. I know riders, from beginners to pros, who have questions about their bodies that they aren't comfortable asking bike shop employees, coaches, or even their gynecologists. We've been conditioned to avoid talking about our "nether regions," and that lack of communication is hurting the cyclist population. There are new riders who are still deciding whether or not to commit to our awesome sport and don't know about bike-specific shorts, and veteran riders who are about to quit because they can't get rid of saddle sores—and that's making riding a whole lot less fun.

Cycling shouldn't be uncomfortable. You shouldn't be getting saddle sores every ride. Your clitoris shouldn't feel numb (and for the gentlemen reading this, nor should your penis). Cramping shouldn't be making you cry on the bike. And you shouldn't be wearing your underwear with your bike shorts.

"A lot of women don't even know that underwear under bike shorts is a no-no. They're like, 'I'm getting this horrible rash where my underwear is,' and I'm like, 'Whoa!'" bike shop manager Samantha Stumpf laughs as we start chatting. It sounds funny to those of us who know not to wear underwear with our shorts.

It was not so funny to me 10 years ago, though, when I was the one on the ride who got pointed at, until a friend finally took me aside and explained that underwear wasn't necessary with bike shorts. The complaint is all too familiar: we aren't told these basic things, yet people assume we have this knowledge that somehow has been passed on, possibly through osmosis. It makes me wonder how many women quit cycling because it's uncomfortable—not because it really is uncomfortable, but because they're missing some basic information.

When I first started riding a bike, I had no idea what a chamois was. I had no idea you shouldn't wear underwear with it—to be honest, I rode in running shorts for the first two years of my cycling career. When a teammate gave me my first set of shorts along with my jersey, I was absolutely perplexed by the pad in them. And when I got a saddle sore, I freaked out a teensy bit. But what I didn't do was talk to anyone about it.

Sure, I'd have my yearly visit to the gynecologist. But if you think I was going to sit down and try to have a real discussion about the state of my ... ahem ... lady parts, well, you are sorely mistaken. For someone as loud-mouthed as I can be, I shut up quick when faced with talking about my *whisper* vagina.

Well, not anymore. Too long have women suffered, faced with awkward questions like, "How do I deal with this saddle sore?" In fact, why aren't women asking, "How can I prevent saddle sores?"

Because no one likes to talk about vaginas, that's why. Because it's awkward, messy, and occasionally hilarious. For me, working in a male-dominated industry, it just feels taboo to mention that I'm having some "female issues" on a ride. Or after a ride. Or right before a ride.

As one of the wonderful women interviewed for this book, Beth Leibo, put it, we need to make women feel like it's OK to say they're uncomfortable, because they are uncomfortable! "We're riding on the most sensitive part of our bodies," she adds.

This is a short guide to being comfortable as a cyclist, and to asking the weird questions. Here, we aren't talking training or bike mechanics (much). We are talking about the issues that people rarely talk about: periods, labia, penises, and a bit about what beginner (and some pro) riders should know to make a bike ride a lot more fun and a lot more comfortable, from the bike shop experience to the bike shorts experience.

"It's disheartening to see new cyclists not having fun," SmartAthlete endurance coach Peter Glassford says, talking about his experience with women who've fallen in and—just as quickly—out of love with cycling, whether it's because they're intimidated by a local fast cycling club, or because of a nagging saddle sore that just won't go away. It shouldn't be like that. "Look for easy group rides that focus on skills, conversation, and learning to ride, rather than just suffering on the bike," he suggests, for starters. "Build those groups. The fun part about cycling is just going out and riding with a couple friends, chatting for a couple hours, practicing skills, playing. The perception of what cycling is for different people is so interesting. No one is wrong, that's the beauty of cycling."

If you're a pro, you might know most of this, and you can feel free to jump around to the issues presented in the book that are pertinent to you—some of the information may seem tedious, but for some women, it's all new.

And for the men reading this, feel free to skip over the chapters on women-specific issues. There's a chapter dedicated to your needs as well, and plenty of the topics covered (shorts, chamois cream, saddles and saddle sores) are just as important for men as they are for women.

To write this book, I started by talking to several different gynecologists, doctors, cyclists, saddle makers, chamois designers, chamois cream creators, bike fitters, women who work in bike shops, coaches who work with junior women and pro women, and even, in one incredibly strange moment, a bikini waxer. I spoke with anyone I thought would have some insight into how to make riding more comfortable. And I asked those questions you've always wanted to ask but didn't feel comfortable bringing up. These people are kick-ass professionals, and many of the ones I spoke with are also cyclists, or spend time with enough cyclists to know what we deal with on the bike.

I asked them some of the questions that I've never felt comfortable asking before: Some questions were from my own personal experience, some are from women who've written and asked me for advice.

Let's stop pretending that riding a bike is easy on our "stuff." It isn't. But we can make it better!

And that starts with stating the problem, and asking for help.

Even in bike shops with female employees, it feels weird to spill your personal business to everyone. But if you were at a gynecologist's office, you would tell your doctor what was up, right? At a nutritionist's office, you would tell him or her what exactly you've been eating, right? There's no reason to feel strange— your main contact point with the bike is, in fact, your pelvic region, and so talking about it in a bike shop shouldn't be a taboo.

"Women come in and they're so excited to see a woman working," Stumpf tells me. Unfortunately, she adds, "It's often basic information that they're missing. In a lot of shops, it's about making the bike sale, but they're not thinking about things that go along with the bike." When you go to buy a bike, ask what else will make the ride more comfortable, and what kind of accessories you need—

and consider a bike fit.

"I'm amazed at how many women are scared to get a fit, or intimidated by the process," Stumpf says. "But it can make such a huge difference to your ride comfort." And that's just one of the hurdles women are facing.

"I believe it is so important for people to have a good source of information, and also to feel comfortable talking to their doctors if they are unsure about something," Esther Yun, one of our gynecologist panelists, said. "Having a good relationship with your gynecologist is important. Believe me, it is excessively difficult to 'gross out' or 'freak out' a gynecologist... Really! Don't be afraid to bring up issues that are important to you, even if they feel small. Small problems can lead to bigger ones if not addressed properly and early!"

The goal here is, as Glassford mentions, to try and cultivate that fun, social part of cycling. "That's the enjoyment and that's how you become a lifelong cyclist," he adds. But that's not easy to do if you can't put your weight on the saddle without wanting to scream in pain, which is where this book comes in.

I hope you learn as much as I did.

YOUR TOP TIPS

As a cyclist for the past decade, I had years to learn my way around dealing with my "chamois area" while on the bike—and off the bike! And I've met plenty of other women who, after a lot of time spent riding together, finally all sat down and talked about what works for us and what doesn't. If you only read one chapter of this book, make it this one. I'll get into most of these topics in depth as the book goes on, but I know you're busy, and I want you to start getting the best results as fast as possible.

A few of the top tips I've picked up:

Invest in a saddle and a good pair of shorts—this is the number one piece of advice from Samantha Stumpf, the soft-goods manager at Park Ave Bike in up-state New York, as well as Beth Leibo, a rep at Assos and a veteran cyclist. One good pair is better than three crappy pairs, any day of the week (though make sure you wash it after every ride!). Brad Sheehan, co-founder and lead designer at Velocio, says, "People don't realize that if you find stuff that fits well, that can make cycling a much more comfortable experience." I could not agree more. Get something that fits well, where the chamois is comfortable and not diaper-like, something that will allow you to go out and do some serious miles. The same is true of your saddle: a saddle that fits your pelvic structure will alleviate pressure and keep you safe from numbness and chafing, and your sit bone width is actually pretty simple to measure.

The one everyone jokes about, but seriously, it's a problem. Repeat after me: **You do not wear underwear with bike shorts** (heretofore referred to as your chamois—pronounce "sham-ee"). This, and I can't emphasize this enough, is bad for you. The chamois is there to pad your seat a bit, but also to keep the bad bacteria away from your genitals. All underwear does is trap the bad stuff in there. Gross.

Speaking of chamois... **Wash your chamois, carefully**. This seems kind of obvious, but just make sure that when you're washing your kit, the inside of the chamois is actually getting clean. Sometimes, it doesn't get as squeaky clean during a wash cycle as you might prefer, especially in a big load of clothes. The second part to this is making sure that your shorts are getting rinsed enough. I've had a lot of people complain about getting rashes from their chamois, and nine times out of ten when I tell them to rinse their shorts an extra time in the wash, that solves the problem. Leftover detergent plus sweaty, exposed skin leads to irritation.

Use chamois cream when needed. Chamois cream fights the friction between your skin and your shorts. Not everyone needs it, and not every ride requires it, but it's helpful, and not something to be afraid of. There are even female-specific ones out there, designed to help balance your pH. If you're going to be out on the bike for a while, definitely apply a bit before you head out the door. At first, it takes some getting used to and feels kind of slippery, but trust me, you'll learn to love it.

Keep it clean. The easiest way to avoid issues like saddle sores and ingrown hairs is by keeping everything clean. For some people, that means simply keeping your nether regions fully hair-free (waxing or shaving is fine—but more on that later). Hair-free means chamois cream can actually get to the skin, not caught up in pubic hair, and that means it can actually do its job, rather than just help to trap bacteria in there. But if you prefer to keep it au naturel, that's totally fine too. You just need to keep things relatively trim (to avoid pulling!) and make sure you do a quick wipe down pre-ride so you're starting with a clean slate.

Be honest with your coach. I don't just mean about if you skipped a workout or if you're having a busy week at the office. I mean, let him or her know when your period is, if cramping is an issue, if you have a bad saddle sore, if you're trying to get pregnant—anything health-related is also going to impact your cycling. Guess what? Your coach will get it. Maybe the week you have your period is a good week to plan as the rest week in the month. Or maybe, if you're having severe cramping, your coach will suggest you go to a gynecologist and discuss your options. A coach wants what's best for you, and if you're not being totally honest, it's impossible for him to do his job. It may feel awkward at first, and you can even mention that it's a hard topic for you to bring up. But if both of you can be on the same page, you'll get the most bang for your coaching buck.

Drop your shorts. I devote a whole chapter to this point because it matters so much when it comes to your in-ride hygiene and ability to avoid saddle sores. If you take nothing else from this book, take away the fact that when you finish a ride, your shorts come off immediately.

Treat early, avoid issues later. A saddle sore is easier to cure when it's first starting (and it's even better if you can prevent it altogether). Catching one early and taking appropriate steps to get rid of it can keep you healthy and even avoid needing surgery! A day off the bike beats a season on the couch.

Lastly, and perhaps most subjectively, my final tip is that embracing your female-ness is OK. To be honest, this is a subject that gets me a lot of angry emails So I will first stress that there is no right or wrong way to be as a female racer. We get caught up in stereotypes all too often, and there are a lot of woman-versus-woman disagreements within the cycling community. At the end of the day, you do you. I get pedicures and manicures on occasion. I have been known to wear mascara on a ride. And sometimes, I don't. And you know what? That's OK. Sometimes, it seems like the cycling industry and the people in the scene have hard-line ideas of what being a racer or a rider is, and those ideals are at odds with what some may consider feminine.

You know what? Screw it. If you want to wear lip gloss, go for it. If you don't, don't. It's easy to get hung up on the politics of femininity and sport, but at the end of the day, do what makes you feel the best.

All right. Now that the basics are covered, on to the tough stuff.

THE ANATOMY OF A BIKE

If you're new to cycling, some of the measurements we talk about when we talk about fit and position in this book may be confusing, so we have this lovely little cheat sheet:

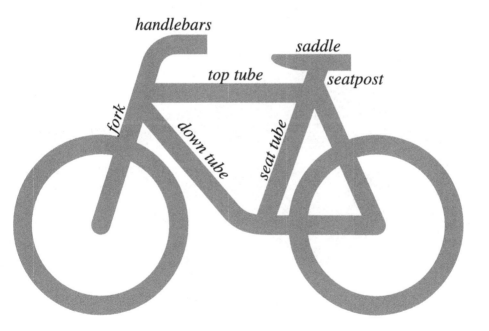

THE ANATOMY OF A SADDLE

What do we mean when we're talking about saddles? For those of you new to cycling, or at least, new to cycling terminology, here's your cheat sheet for this book.

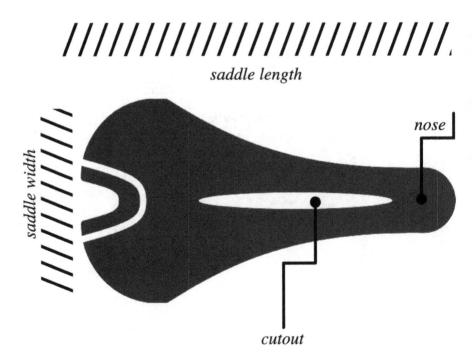

saddle length

saddle width

nose

cutout

FINDING YOUR SADDLE SOULMATE

Finding a saddle is a lot like getting onto a dating website—a lot of options might look good, but end up being truly terrible for you. And, unfortunately, until you go on that first date (or ride, in this case), you won't know how it's going to feel.

"Saddles are like jeans," shop worker Samantha Stumpf explains. "You go into a store and try on 20 pairs of jeans and think, 'Oh God, one has to fit.'"

"First, I ask what kind of riding women are planning on doing, and try to work out if they have problems with pressure or chafing or rubbing," she says. "If a rider is having those issues, it's usually that the nose of the saddle is too wide, or the width of the saddle for their sit bones isn't correct. And that's a measurement that can feel pretty awkward to take, but it shouldn't."

Picking a saddle can be a nightmare. It's arguably harder than picking a bike, or tires, or any other component because it's the one that you're most intimate (for lack of a better word) with. It's the part of the bike that you're connected to the closest, and it may take a few tries before you find your saddle soulmate.

"The biggest problem is that women just accept the stock saddle that comes on the bike," says Lisa Wilkes, head of customer service at Terry Bicycles.

"If your saddle is annoying you to the point where it is a limiter on a ride, then that is the limiter we need to be working on. If you don't mention it because it's an embarrassing area on your body, that is a huge disservice to you, your coach, and your performance," coach Peter Glassford explains. "Not adjusting things to improve a saddle sore situation can affect your whole season, if not more.

Cycling is hard enough without constant pain: Get help! We can try things like a day off, a day cross-training, different saddles, bike fits, chamois creme, mobility work, and different types of riding."

This sounds overwhelming, because it is. "It can be daunting when you walk in a bike shop and there's so much choice," says Paula Dyba. "And as a new rider, it's hard to articulate what you want and need. You end up defaulting to what feels soft when you press it or what someone standing next to you recommends. But a little education is a good thing."

She adds that trying a couple saddles is great, but that can be daunting to someone who's new to riding—even changing the saddle on the bike can be difficult! If you're testing out new saddles at a shop, before you leave, make sure someone in the shop has shown you how to swap out your old saddle for the new one, and how to adjust not just the height, but the fore and aft—how far forward or backward your saddle is.

THE DIFFERENCE BETWEEN MEN AND WOMEN

"Whether your saddle is made for a woman or not, everyone is going to have a certain way that they sit on a bike, set up a bike, pedal a bike, and will have different injuries, so it makes sense that different saddles will be better for being more comfortable for different riders," Glassford notes. That might mean you need a cutout; that might mean you are entirely more comfortable on a saddle designed "for men." Guess what? No one's nether regions are the same.

This isn't just anecdotal. In 2008, a study published in the *Official Journal of the American College of Sports Medicine* entitled "Gender Differences in Bicycle Saddle Pressure Distribution during Seated Cycling" concluded that, "There are significant gender-related differences in saddle loading [where your weight rests on the saddle], which are important to consider when designing saddles. These differences are especially important when riders are in the handlebar drops and more weight is supported on the anterior pelvic structures." That means that the saddle your husband swears by may be terrible for you—we simply have different structures.

Companies are taking note of this, and adjusting their saddles to make women's versions. "We approach saddle and chamois development with the same general principles in mind, specifically the anatomy of both men and women as well as how riders tend to sit on their bike," says Bontrager's Jesse Bartholomew. "Our inForm biodynamics team lead by Kyle Russ is constantly pursuing new research and development efforts to better understand these variables, but our chamois and saddle designs represent the cutting edge of this work."

"Considering the differences between men and women, we can really only generalize," says Bontrager's Russ. "It's very possible that pelvic bone structures ind angles of pubic rami land in between one of our sizes and a men's saddle can work better for a women or vice versa. In general, however, this is relatively are."

An incorrectly-sized saddle for your sit bones can have serious in-ride repercussions—saddle width is an important determinant for finding a few saddles to try initially. "While the chamois primarily provides cushioning, the saddle needs to provide real support for the rider's bone structure," says Russ. "This is why the chamois doesn't need to be sized, but saddles most definitely do. In addition to the sizing being different between men's and women's saddles, generally speaking, the comfort relief zones and cut outs are bigger and wider on women's saddles to provide soft tissue pressure relief, and the saddle nose is wider on women's saddles to accommodate the shallow pubic rami angle."

Sadly, when Ergon's ergonomics designer Janine Haas did her master's thesis on this very topic, it was inconclusive as to what kind of saddle women need. So there won't be a perfect saddle by the end of this chapter.

The recently-published study done by Haas at the German Sport University in Cologne reads: "Sitting discomfort is widely-spread along the [female] participants of the questionnaire. 73.5 percent were showing complaints which were mostly affecting the genital area."

That is a HUGE number. Three in four women on your group ride are uncomfortable with their saddles.

Haas's research showed that too much pressure was the primary cause of discomfort. But there are saddles that can reduce that pressure. For example, she cites the Terry Butterfly saddle saying that the saddle is designed to reduce pressure in the back portion of the saddle.

But pressure from the saddle affects people differently. "For some cyclists, gender-specific constructional features might be an appropriate solution, for others it is unhelpful," she says. "Additional factors influencing the pressure distribution on a saddle have to be identified in further studies in order to improve the choice of an individually-suited saddle model to improve sitting comfort."

So, in simpler terms, a female-specific saddle may not work for you—and for the male riders out there, that female-specific saddle might actually be perfect. It just depends.

"The female pelvis is wider, so the sit bones have a greater distance from each other," Haas explains. "They're a little wider since we need to give birth. So, the sit bones are wider and the pelvic bones are wider and also more curved than the male pubic bones."

"That means a woman's bony structures are going to be more laterally placed on the saddle. The male pelvis is thinner but also longer, so when a male sits on the saddle, he needs less space," she adds. "When you have a typical woman's pelvis, the saddle needs to be a bit wider than a male saddle, and needs a little more space in the middle part of the saddle so when you go to the drops and your pelvis rolls to the front, the saddle is still wide enough."

"There are differences everywhere, so it may be that a woman is more comfortable on a male-specific saddle, or a man is more comfortable on a women's saddle," Haas says. "Typically, a female pelvis is wider though, and the skin is a bit softer and thinner. Because of that, women may be more sensitive to pressure than men are, especially where you are on the saddle, and in the drops in particular. It's definitely very important that your saddle is wide enough, but then look at the features—are you more comfortable on a flat saddle, or do you need one with more of a curve to support your bony structures and not irritate your skin? There are a lot of saddles with a special relief area, like a cutout in the middle. It's hard to say what's the best for you without trying a few."

"Because of the anatomy of the female pelvis, pressure is distributed slightly unevenly compared to the male pelvis," she added. "There are three points where pressure appears. You want a saddle to centralize pressure in an area that can handle the pressure."

For men, the pressure is in a different place than it is for a woman, so the contact points on a saddle are different, explains Paula Dyba, the Marketing VP and Creative Director at Terry Bicycles. "For women, our cutaways are moved forward and for men, they're moved back. For men, the recess in the rear is deeper, and the width of the saddle is a bit narrower in the rear," she adds. "Men's sit bones are about half an inch narrower than women's on average."

And while a cutout in the saddle may seem to be an ideal solution for relieving pressure, that isn't always the case. A study in the *Journal of Sexual Medicine* entitled "Women's bike seats: A pressing matter for competitive female cyclists," suggested that cutouts are a bad choice, especially if you have a lot of pressure sensitivity. "Cut-out and narrower saddles negatively affect saddle pressures in female cyclists," the study concluded.

That's because a hole in a saddle doesn't really provide relief on the soft tissue as much as a bit of flexibility in the saddle and a bit of ventilation, says Dyba. Still, a cutout may be more comfortable for you.

PICKING YOUR SADDLE

If you're trying to decide on a saddle, the best measurement that you can start with is the width of your sit bones. "One thing that you can measure is sit bone distance so you know what width you're looking for," says Haas. Most bike shops can help you with this, thanks to specially made 'ass-o-meters' that you sit on to leave indentations where your sit bones rest. The measurements of your sit bone width helps dictate the size of the saddle you want, but don't panic if your sit bones are 'small' or 'large.' It's just about the bones you were born with, and you can't change that measurement with diet or exercise.

When searching for the perfect saddle, Haas also notes that, "It's pretty important to know which bike you want to ride and how you're going to ride it when choosing a saddle." That means what works on your mountain bike may not work for your road bike, since you ride each differently—so don't assume what feels great on one bike will automatically be awesome on the other.

It's tempting to go for a 'car-seat' saddle when thinking about comfort. But a wide rear on the saddle isn't always good: if you have closer-spaced sit bones, a wide saddle may actually make you feel like your sit bones are being pulled apart slightly. You want your sit bones to support your weight primarily, and balance that with your feet on the pedals and your hands on the handlebars. With a saddle wider than your sit bones, your soft tissue, rather than the sit bones, will be taking the brunt of the pressure as you pedal.

Additionally, don't forget to look at the width of the nose of the saddle, since it is often a source of chafing that is not considered when picking a saddle, says Dyba. "That's so critical. Anything too wide in the nose is going to be painful from that standpoint, so we don't mess with the width of the nose, no matter what we do in the back of the saddle with the width."

It's not all about the saddle though—overall bike fit can play a major role as well, as shown in a 2012 study published in *The Journal of Sexual Medicine* entitled "The Bar Sinister: Does Handlebar Level Damage the Pelvic Floor in Female Cyclists?" The article concluded that handlebars positioned lower than the saddle were significantly associated with increased perineum saddle pressures and decreased genital sensation in female cyclists. Adjusting your bike's handlebar height might completely change how your nether regions feel!

And lastly, you have to consider your pelvic tilt, especially as a female rider. A 2007 study published by the American College of Sports Medicine entitled "Influence of Gender, Power, and Hand Position on Pelvic Motion during Seated Cycling" concluded that there is substantial pelvic motion during seated cycling. Experienced female road cyclists exhibited greater average anterior tilt than their male counterparts, and that pelvic motion seems to arise naturally during seated cycling and should be considered when designing women's saddles.

So, when you go for a bike fit—and note that I say *when* and not *if*—since that's the best way to get comfortable on a bike and the right position—make sure to ask about your pelvic tilt.

What does this all boil down to?

Simply put, try a whole bunch of saddles, from ones made specifically for women, to aggressive men's racing saddles. Most shops have ways for clients to demo saddles, and most teams and clubs have a few lying around to share. If you have friends with similar builds to yours, ask them about favorite saddles—but don't take what they say as the only possibility. Keep an open mind, and keep trying new options. The perfect saddle is out there, and it will make riding a whole lot better.

YOUR BIKE FIT

You may have gone through 20 saddles and still can't get comfortable. But before you go for number 21, consider getting a bike fit—or re-fit, if you've already had one. The odds are good that your fit is wrong, if you're still struggling after trying a few different types of saddles.

"When I was the head coach of Team in Training, I'd get riders who had really never been on a bike. And they didn't want to raise their seats to the right level because they were scared of it. Finding ways to build women's confidence on the bike is huge," says Lisa Wilkes, head of customer service at Terry Bicycles. Starting with a bike fit is the best way to make the transition from timid new rider to confident hill climber, and a good bike fit can make you more comfortable than any saddle on a poorly fit bike can.

"The absolute best way to buy a saddle and chamois is to start with a bike fit from a reputable bike fitter," says Kyle Russ, a Trek Precision Fitter. "Many saddle and chamois problems can actually have their root cause in poor bike fit."

There are different levels of bike fit, from the pricier multiple hour sessions with a fitter, to a quick fit (or 'sizing') in a shop ideally taking your sit bones and saddle choice into account. You have to decide what's best for you, but if you've had consistent pain or numbness for a long time, a more extensive bike fit is worth investing in.

"Sometimes, I can adjust the nose of a saddle by just one degree, and it changes everything," says Stephen LeBoyer, owner and head fitter at Savile Road in upstate New York. He says that he sees so many riders who've just never considered fitting their bikes, despite riding in clearly uncomfortable situations. "I had a woman the other day, the nose of her saddle was pointing up 45 degrees, while she's riding in the drops. I thought, 'That's got to hurt!' I asked her casually if there was a reason her saddle was at that angle, and she replied, 'No, it just went on that way.'"

But a bike fit doesn't just make you comfortable, he adds. A bike fit helps your body do the job it needs to do, and can completely change how well you ride.

Getting a fit? Before you make an appointment, make sure you're prepared and know what to expect.

CHOOSE WISELY

"Fitters and fitting in general aren't regulated: there's no real barrier to entry," LeBoyer says. So the first thing to understand is that there's no guarantee that a local fitter is a good fitter. So many people—coaches and shop employees and mechanics—have just enough knowledge about fitting to be dangerous. "Measurements are great to have as a frame of reference, but they're just that: reference points and starting points," he says, and adds that even after decades of fit experience, he's still learning—as should all fitters. Interview a bike fitter before you hop on the bike with him or her!

YOU SHOULD BE COMFORTABLE

There just shouldn't be pain while you're riding, LeBoyer explains (at least, not pain in your nether regions. Your legs probably burn sometimes.). "When I do a fit for someone who's been having that pain, it's like an 'aha' moment during a fit, because we adjust for that and address that pain."

YOUR FIT SHOULD START OFF THE BIKE

Many quality fits start off the bike with assessment of your movement and range of motion—as an example, Trek Precision's bike fit process starts on a massage table, running through a series of movements to show the fitters your flexibility ranges. During that, the fitter should be interviewing you about your medical and injury history, your past riding, and your goals.

"I start with an interview," says LeBoyer. "I want to know what kind of rider you are, what goals you have, how much you're riding, what kind of riding you're doing. If you're a mountain biker, I want to know if you're casually riding or if you're trying to place in Leadville. I want to know how you got in the position on your bike that you're in now, if you've had fit experience. I want to know about injuries, broken bones, medications that you're on."

AVOID ANYONE WHO SAYS "ALL WOMEN..."

"I don't group people by gender, I look at individuals," LeBoyer says. That's smart, since not all women are the same, and generalizing about our bodies won't lead anywhere good. "Women-specific geometry can be great and it works well for a lot of women, but there are also some women who do better with men's frames." He adds that you have to look at fitting as an individual result. For example, what works for one woman who's been riding for a decade may not work for her identical twin sister who hasn't been riding or isn't as fit, despite sharing the same bone structure.

REFLECT ON YOUR PAIN

Before you go in, know what your problems are. "When you go to a fitting, know what doesn't work," says LeBoyer. "If you're in the hoods, does it feel good, but then in the drops, you're getting too much pressure in the soft tissue? Think about that before you go to the fit and make a checklist of what you don't like and what you like."

A BIKE FIT CAN'T REPLACE PHYSICAL THERAPY

"I do a range of motion test to see how flexible you are. If you can't touch your toes, I need to know that before I fit you," says LeBoyer. "If you go and get fit and no one checks your cleat placement, no one asks if you've been injured, no one asks about your flexibility, something is missing."

At Trek, Russ explains that often, they'll fit someone for the bike, but also recommend physical therapy to address some of the pain and flexibility issues they see. A bike fit isn't a miracle drug, sadly.

"If you're getting lower back pain or knee discomfort, and it happens every day, figure out if it's bike-specific. Is it specific to one bike, like your road bike, or is it every time you ride any bike or do any other activity? If it's one bike, that's a fit issue. If it's all the time, then it's more likely a back problem that you need to figure out," LeBoyer says.

Share Your Goals

"Regardless of what kind of fitting we're doing, the interview process remains the same. But fit varies depending on what you're doing, for example, the difference between a road bike and a cyclocross bike, or a road bike for a criterium versus a long-course triathlon," says LeBoyer. Even though the frames and geometries are similar, angles will change to more or less aggressive depending on the goals. If you're planning to take on an Ironman, make sure your fitter knows that's the goal, versus a sprint race.

Fit Frequently

Most people should get a new fit every couple years. "We age. We're not getting more flexible. And typically, we're not getting much fitter as we get older," says LeBoyer. "Plus, people lose or gain weight and even a little can change your fit. And a fitting doesn't even necessarily mean changing things—it might mean small adjustments."

Get a Second Opinion

Got a fit and still not feeling great? You can always get another, from someone else. "Think about it like a doctor. Talk to the fitter, get a second opinion, get recommendations from friends on fitters," says LeBoyer. Above all, you need to feel confident in their advice.

THE ANATOMY OF THE CHAMOIS

All right. You've found a good saddle. But without a comfortable pair of bike shorts or bibs, the perfect saddle still won't guard against chafing, infections, or saddle sores. That's where a great pair of shorts truly shines—and where an ill-fitting pair can wreck a ride. And the shorts and saddle need to be viewed as a unit: a bad saddle or a bad chamois, or just the wrong combination, can make a ride a lot less comfortable.

"The saddle is the support structure for the bone and the chamois works with the saddle to reduce peak pressure," explains Kyle Russ, a Biomechanical Engineer at Trek. And the padding on both, when put together, can be the perfect combination... Or an utter disaster. "If there is too much padding, it can actually increase the amount of pressure or put pressure in areas not intended by either chamois or saddle designers," Russ adds.

That's why, for both saddles and chamois, you want enough padding to reduce peak pressure without wedging into sensitive tissues, bunching, or general discomfort, adds Bontrager's Jason Fryda.

Again, shorts are like saddles in that some of them simply won't fit you right, while they work great for a friend. "There's not one type of rider so there's not one shorts concept that's going to work," says Paula Dyba, the Marketing VP and Creative Director at Terry Bicycles.

Some chamois will be too bulky; others will be too thin. Some will have seams in spots that chafe for you, and different styles suit different body types better. You'll probably have to try a few pairs before you find your favorite, but there are a few things you should look for: good, solid construction, a leg gripper you find comfortable, and a chamois that's more than just a piece of foam padding carelessly stuffed into the crotch of a pair of spandex shorts.

"Of all three parts that touch the bike—our feet, our hands and our nether regions—our nether regions are the most important!" says veteran rider and Assos rep Beth Leibo. "Shorts can really make or break your ride. This is one of those things I would really drive home: Women have a much harder time being comfortable on a saddle because we can't push things to the side. No one talks about that!" Preach it, Leibo.

And because of that, she argues, "It's even more of a priority for a woman to be more comfortable and have a good chamois. Getting one pair of bike shorts or bibs that has a female-specific chamois can prevent any kind of soreness, numbness, saddle sores, ongoing chafing, anything like that at all. Chamois cream is a backup, but you shouldn't need it."

Don't think that you can grab a pair of men's shorts and be comfortable, either. Good shorts are differently padded for males and females. "The padding shape is very gender-specific because of the differences in angle of the pubic rami and differences in soft tissue," explains Russ.

Strange but true: Women's chamois, by design, tend to look more phallic, while a chamois designed to comfortably cradle a penis and testicles (and keep them out of harm's way) actually more closely resemble the female anatomy, and have a channel for the male 'parts' to rest.

So, paradoxically, Leibo says if you want to see if your chamois was specifically designed for a woman, turn the shorts inside out and take a look. "It almost looks like an erect penis," she laughs. "And the mens' often have a slit in the middle."

This is because women's shorts are designed so that when you lean forward, the chamois takes away pressure from that part of the body and dissipates the pressure. "It's a whole pad on the front when you lean forward," she says, so when you tilt your pelvis, you still have some cushion.

"We're taught not to mention these things, not to talk about these things, and then to go into a bike shop and try to explain something like this to an 18-year-old guy," says Leibo, and that's just not going to work.

When you're going to buy a pair of shorts, think of them as just as important as your bike, and don't just grab the first pair you find on a rack. Brad Sheehan, co-founder and lead designer at Velocio, says to look for quality, not quantity. "I'm biased, of course, but I'd say across the board in cycling, from apparel to equipment, my best advice is to buy the best quality you can afford. You're going to enjoy it more, it'll perform better, and you'll want to ride more. And that's obviously the whole point," he explains.

"A pair of bib shorts is one of the most significant purchases you'll make in terms of your comfort: it's the main contact point, it's the highest friction point with the bike, and it's going to provide support for the biggest muscles you're going to use on the bike. There are more benefits to good shorts than any other piece of clothing," Sheehan concludes.

For Velocio, creating women's chamois was simple: they started from the women's line and moved into men's gradually, but as Sheehan notes, this wasn't a brand that was 'shrinked and pinked.' "We wanted to turn that typical mens-to-womens design process upside down and really went to the fundamentals of how to design and cut patterns and choose materials that were centered around women's anatomy and their wants and needs, all produced at a really high level. We wanted to adjust this end of the market: We know women's cycling is a segment that's growing constantly. You see that in big bike brands. Now, there are female equivalent versions to the top men's bikes out there, and that's in line with what we saw happening when we started."

They aren't the only ones. At Terry, Paula Dyba, the Marketing VP and Creative Director, says, "We've gone crazy with different types of shorts now: We have a chamois program that's the heart and soul, and that's something that's unique to Terry with how the chamois is constructed. Ours has what we call soft wings, so the foam on the chamois is just through the rear and the nose. On the sides, where it doesn't come in contact with your body, it's just that fabric, but no bulk. You feel that when you're pedaling—excess foam makes a ride uncomfortable, and can actually cause chafing."

The ultimate goal in getting a good pair of shorts or bibs is all open to perception. It's personal preference. "Some women are bold and can ride in a piece of sandpaper and be fine," says Leibo. "But for most women, beginners and intermediate, it's much more advantageous to invest at first in a good short."

What you're looking for, in addition to a chamois you find comfortable, is a chamois that has an antimicrobial coating on the material and the foam. "Assos, for example, is designed first and foremost to take pressure away from the area, but in conjunction with that, it's trying to keep everything as dry as it can possibly stay," says Leibo. "And that's a factor where the antimicrobial design comes in—so everything stays dry and doesn't create more bacteria."

Dyba adds that you want to look for a short with perforations in the chamois to keep the ventilation and wick moisture.

To find the perfect pair of shorts, Leibo recommends first finding a store you're comfortable in, that has a decent selection of women's clothing. "If you can get a female employee to talk about the best chamois for the style of riding that a rider is going to do, that's the best of both worlds."

She also recommends investing in yourself: "An entry level short is just that—a step up from a pair of underwear and a pair of cotton shorts, but if you invest in a nicer, higher level pair, that will be the pair you go back to. If you get four to six hours to be on your bike a week, you want everything to be comfortable and to work and to promote you getting back on the bike. That's the ultimate goal. The more fun you have, the more you'll ride."

Because shorts can be pricey—anywhere from $50 for a cheaper pair up to $400 for some of the top-of-the-line models, Leibo says starting with just one good pair of shorts is better than buying a few pairs of cheaper ones. "You can wash a pair of shorts after a spin class, just hand-wash or wash them in the shower, turn them inside out, hang them up, and an hour later, they're dry and you can go for a ride in the afternoon," she says. "But nothing like that is communicated to women."

"Cheap shorts tend to have narrow, elasticized waistbands," says Dyba. That means they tend to be much more uncomfortable. "Better ones will have flat, yoga-style fronts and no elastic in the front so when you bend over, it won't pinch. Cheap chamois are something to dodge—you have to pay attention to that."

A cheap pair of shorts is also likely to have a lower quality chamois. Sheehan explains that the cheaper pads are made of thermo-pressed foam, and they can be made into a variety of shapes and the designs are built in. "They're really technical looking," he explains, but that doesn't make them better. "Then, you have stitched pads, which are what we use at Velocio. It's a lot simpler looking. The foams are stitched on to the top layer of fabric."

He adds, "The difference is that the stitched pads tend to be more flexible, since when you apply heat to foam, it doesn't stretch as much and there are slight ridges. With a stitched chamois, you don't have those edges and the high density foams we use tend to be more flexible."

With a stitched padding, Sheehan adds, "You can pinpoint where you want the high density foam and where you want the low density foam. You want shapes that work with the anatomy and have flexibility in terms of size, saddle choice and positioning, so you're working in a range, not trying to make the tolerances so tight that they only work for a tiny percentage of the population."

Looking at a chamois that feels like a diaper? Put it back. "Soft squishy foam is going to bottom out and not do anything," says Sheehan. "You want a higher density foam."

Cheap shorts might seem like a great deal, but once you wash them a few times, you'll likely see why they were on the bargain rack to begin with: higher quality shorts stand up better to frequent washings, while a cheap chamois tends to deform and lose its shape after a few rides. If you think about the cost of a higher-quality pair, you'll quickly realize that one great pair of shorts is actually cheaper than buying an inexpensive pair, in the long run.

And for every rider—male or female—most cyclists who've been riding for years will say that their best recommendation is to try out bib shorts. Those are the shorts with suspenders instead of a waistband, and they're often more comfortable than similar shorts models. "The second you put on a pair of bib shorts, regardless of the percentage of body fat you have, you feel thinner," says Leibo. "It essentially takes away that elasticity between the most sensitive part of your body. You don't want that muffin-top popping out, or shorts cutting off your breathing."

Bibs, on the other hand, help you breathe better because there's no tight band. "You feel better, and you feel more comfortable. It helps hold in everything, from the girls to the belly," Leibo adds. "I would argue that if just one in five women would wear bibs, there would be so many more women cyclists!"

"But how do I pee in bib shorts?" You're probably asking that right now if you're not already wearing them. Well, now there are shorts being made to pee in, with halter harnesses, clip-on straps, and even zippers in the back. Velocio has a bib short with a zipper, and it works great.

"We've pushed that and tried to innovate with things like the Signature Fly Bib Short that addressed the need to make it easier for women to use the bathroom in bib shorts," says Sheehan. "We started working on that right when we started Velocio because we knew if we did it right, it was a game-changer. We knew we needed to do it right, and not compromise fit and performance though. We went through half a dozen concepts and ideas before we settled on it."

Whether you're shopping for bibs or shorts, though, size matters—and can make any shorts, no matter how cheap or pricey, feel awful. "People tend to buy bibs a little too big because when you try them on, at first they feel a little tight," says Sheehan. "But there's a bit of a break-in period after they're washed and soften up a bit. If there's extra material, if they're not compressive, you're not getting the full benefit of the shorts."

Oftentimes, people think a chamois needs to be really big. But the chamois doesn't need to be any bigger than your saddle. That's where it's supporting you. What is important is the positioning of the pad in the shorts. "You see a lot of people riding and you can see a third of the chamois sticking out over the back of the saddle," says Sheehan. "That's not doing anything, if it's halfway up your butt! If it fits like that, it's too far back."

So, to summarize: invest in yourself. And by yourself, I mean shorts that you love, that fit great, that make you feel awesome, and that stay in place and feel comfortable, even after a couple hours in the saddle. And try different types—especially bibs and newer shorts that feature a softer, wider yoga-pant-style band on the top.

THE 3 CHAMOIS FACTORS

If you're not sure what to look for in a chamois, Bontrager's Senior Product Manager Jason Fryda has a few factors you should look at as you're chamois-shopping. You may not see this info on the labels, but compare the different chamois in a few shops (do the bounce test by pressing in the chamois and seeing how it puffs back up, test out densities, and ask shop workers questions about things like the breath-ability).

1. **Longevity**: Higher quality foams just last longer. They are designed to compress and rebound more so they will have the same ride after a few years of regular riding. If you're planning on buying one pair and using them for a long time, you want a pair of shorts with the highest quality foam you can find.

2. **Duration/Comfort**: You want a chamois that can hold up to a long ride, but that doesn't mean a diaper-style puffy pad. Higher quality foams can support, cushion and do so for a few hours without packing down.

3. **Flexibility/Breath-ability**: If you ride for a longer time, moisture can start to really wreak havoc on your saddle comfort and that is where flexibility ensures the chamois stays moving with you, rather than against you, which causes friction. And the higher quality foams will have open cell structures that are more breathable.

READER QUESTION: CHAMOIS SHOPPING TIPS

Heading into the store to shop for pants can be intimidating at the best of times. Going into a store to shop for spandex that's meant to be ultra-form-fitting? Yikes. Any tips for what I should look for in the fitting room?

I know exactly what you mean! First of all, be prepared to try on a lot of shorts before you find the best ones. And when you go, opt for wearing the most seamless underwear possible, since once you're riding, you won't be wearing any, and you want to know how the shorts fit au naturel. Paula Dyba, the Marketing VP and Creative Director at Terry Bicycles, is also here to help with the three things to look for when trying on bike shorts. The first step? Grab a few pairs, and don't be intimidated by shop workers. Strut to the fitting room and get ready to test drive some chamois.

Chamois quality: You want one with a high quality foam—it should feel like it's going to stretch with your body—and you should be able to see that it's perforated for breath-ability.

The fit of the leg bands: This can drive everybody nuts, so it's a big one. It should stay in place but not give you a "sausage" look and feel on your leg. There's a lot of irritation that can come from silicon, so if you're sensitive, consider skipping that latex against your leg: there are plenty of alternative options.

Getting in position: Does the waistband feel good, and do the shorts fit when you're bent over? They need to be tight enough so they're not bagging and won't catch on the saddle. You want a bit of compression... but not too much! And, of course, as you bend over, you should check the opacity of the shorts in natural light—cheap shorts might be thin, so dodge ones with low Lycra content.

PEEING IN BIB SHORTS

The biggest question I hear when riders consider swapping to bib shorts is, "How am I going to pee?" And, to be honest, it is a bit trickier in bibs than it is in shorts. But there are a few hacks and methods that can make it easier.

THE SQUAT-AND-PULL

This is the method most pro racers opt for. It's not the best one for your chamois, since it does involve putting a lot of stretch into your shorts, but it gets the job done. Simply squat low to the ground (hidden from sight, of course), and pull one leg of your shorts up and over to the side, getting your chamois out of the way before you let it go. This method is probably the messiest/most likely to end with pee on your shoes, but it works in any shorts. (Note: a baby wipe makes this a lot less yucky, so if you're often stopping mid-ride to pee, bring one along.)

THE BIBS-DESIGNED-FOR-THIS

There are now a ton of great bib shorts on the market, from Velocio to SheBeest to Giro to Sugoi (just to name a couple) that offer different zipper and snap configurations to allow you to drop your shorts. Velocio's bibs zip down the back so you can pull your shorts down, Giro and SheBeest offer halters that can be pulled off without taking off your jersey, and Sugoi has a snap configuration on the front suspenders to pull them up and over. But don't settle for shorts just because of this feature, look for a pair that's truly comfortable for you!

THE TAKE-IT-ALL-OFF

If you prefer to hit up actual restrooms, then you probably have a few seconds to take off your jersey and pull down your shorts. But the best pro tip here is to swap any half-zip jerseys for full-zip versions so the jersey comes off like a jacket for on/off ease. Otherwise, you'll be dropping stuff on the floor (and in the toilet) as you struggle to pull a jersey over your head.

THE ONE-SHOULDER

This method looks a little TLC-in-the-90s, but it works pretty darn well. Under your jersey, leave one suspender of the bibs down for your ride. Then, when you need to go, you just pull down and over. Like the Squat-and-Pull, though, this adds wear-and-tear to your shorts, especially the suspender elastic. And some people eschew this method because the shorts get slightly out of place when not being held up evenly on both shoulders.

In short, play around and find what works for you, but comfort on the bike—in your nether regions and on your stomach—is well worth a bit of a hassle when nature calls.

PLUS SIZE CONSIDERATIONS

I dislike the term plus size, but it doesn't seem like the industry has found a better option yet. So, my apologies to anyone who dislikes the terminology. But I didn't want to skip over some issues that come up for bigger riders and the questions being brought up at the clinics I have done across North America in the past couple years. Not only is it tougher to find great shorts, it can be tricky navigating saddle choice and dealing with issues like thigh rub.

"You would think with the weight stats out there, shops would want to carry more clothing for bigger sizes," says Lisa Wilkes, head of customer service at Terry Bicycles. Terry is one of the companies that has great options for larger riders—and not just oversized cheap shorts. Their highest quality shorts are made in large sizes, too.

Before dealing with shorts choice, though, riders should consider a proper saddle fit. The problem riders often have is that, as larger women, the assumption is that a wider saddle is better. But weight and pants size have little to do with sit bone width—as an example, my 250 pound, 5'11" father and I (at half the weight and 8 inches shorter) have the same sit bone width and can swap saddles—so take the time to get your sit bones measured before choosing the widest option in the shop.

"In terms of the design process at Terry, typically the first thing we do is try to figure out what women are still having problems with, because there are still a lot of difficult problems out there," says Paula Dyba, the Marketing VP and Creative Director at Terry Bicycles. "The racer women tend to have a different set of problems and tolerances than the everyday or new cyclist. The new cyclist normally goes to thicker, wider, softer with saddle and chamois choice, but the education process needs to start there: that's not always the answer."

"Bigger riders gravitate towards bigger, wider, cushier saddles but, while that may get them on the bike and feel plush for a few pedal strokes, it usually ends in discomfort that makes them stop riding," she continues. "A bad experience for a newer rider can completely send them away from the sport. But swapping to a narrow, properly-sized saddle can seem intimidating or scary."

So don't be afraid of a narrower saddle—be afraid of the car seat-sized ones that will end up numbing your butt after 15 minutes.

Saddles are key, but you also need to find a chamois that works for you—keeping in mind that your chamois shouldn't be hitting your thighs too much or spilling up your back, and should be tight but not so your breathing is restricted.

When you're choosing a jersey, remember: you don't have to wear the same ultra-tight spandex that your friend wears. If you want to, 100 percent go for it. But know that there are many other options out there, and you can find something that makes you comfortable and that looks flattering. (Well, as flattering as spandex is on anyone.) "A lot of women are self-conscious about their midsection, no matter how small they are—those ultra-tight jerseys can be a turn-off," says Wilkes. "I like a relaxed fit jersey: I find it makes a lot of women feel better and more comfortable on the bike."

A reader emailed to ask me: "I'm a plus-sized rider, and I constantly have problems with chafing on my upper legs. Help!"

I asked several riders for their takes on this issue: it's not just restricted to curvier women, since most powerful cyclists have quads so big that a thigh gap isn't happening for them either.

If you do have chafing on your upper thighs, consider a few things:

—Investigate your chamois. Are you chafing because it's a cheap chamois with strings and unfinished seams on the edges that are causing the friction? If so, upgrade to a more seamless design. You also might want to look for shorts with a smaller, designed-for-a-woman chamois.

—Add chamois cream. Go a bit farther down with the chamois cream than you normally would, hitting the spots that are feeling the most friction.

—Try a saddle with a thinner nose. You might just need a bit more wiggle room at the front of the saddle, especially if you have a larger, more padded one now.

What's the Deal with Chamois Cream?

One of the questions I often hear is, "Why use chamois cream?" Another one is, "OK, so how do I use chamois cream?" It's a bit of a head-scratcher for new cyclists, who often either skip chamois cream altogether or overdo it to such an extent that, instead of helping, the cream ends up creating a slip-and-slide in their shorts.

Chamois cream is there to help reduce friction. "There are scenarios of excessive ride length or if you ramp up your mileage abruptly, or you're in environments that are really humid and hot where you might use a cream to manage the dryness," says Jason Fryda, Senior Product Manager at Bontrager. For those of us who know cool and dry is the best way to avoid saddle sores, that seems counter-intuitive, but a cream is much better than sweat on a hot day.

First and foremost, even chamois cream makers will tell you that chamois cream is optional, and shouldn't be necessary for short rides—even long rides, if you have the perfect saddle and shorts combination, should be possible without the friction-fighting agent. But if you need that extra bit of help to decrease friction, chamois cream is great.

A word about the history of the chamois, before we get into how chamois cream works now. Experienced riders may remember a time when bike shorts actually had a leather insert rather than the antimicrobial foam we're used to today. That's where the term chamois comes from, and despite the fact that it's no longer technically accurate, it's still how we refer to our shorts today. Chamois cream, then, was originally designed and used to soften that leather, because let's be honest, who wants to sit on new leather all day?

It was also used to essentially grease-up the rider's "chamois area" enough that friction with the pad wasn't an issue. As time wore on and chamois became what they are today, the point of chamois cream became less about conditioning the shorts and more about protecting the rider from friction.

Enter Steve Mathews, the inventor of Chamois Butt'r and head of Paceline Products. He was a serious racer at the time when all of this technology was changing in the late 80s. "What I picked up from the pro guys back then was that guys were using stuff like Noxema and Vaseline back when we were riding with real leather," Mathews says.

The invention of Chamois Butt'r came after trying many products and finding that, while some of them were effective, the greasy residue left from them was wreaking havoc on his and his wife's laundry cycles. A water-based product was clearly necessary, and he eventually created the formula for the original Chamois Butt'r.

Fast-forward twenty years, and Chamois Butt'r is one of the most well-known brands on the chamois market, and they make so much of it that it's now outsourced to a cosmetics factory. A full collection has evolved from the original cream: Chamois Butt'r, Eurostyle, and Butt'r Her' are all different versions of that same water-based product that he created years ago, but with a few tweaks. The Eurostyle cream features added ingredients like menthol and witch hazel for a natural cooling and cleaning effect, while the Her' cream is pH-balanced (more on that later) with lavender and tea tree oil to do the same cool/clean as the Eurostyle version.

Of course, other brands have made it into the market, including Petal Power and DZ Nuts, and more are introduced every year.

Without the leather chamois as an issue anymore, what's left is a need to prevent chafing from friction, since what happens when you get chafed is that it creates an opening for bacteria to get in, and then you have problems. "But if you lubricate, you don't chafe, and you won't have nearly as many problems," Mathews explains.

DO YOU PUT CHAMOIS CREAM ON SKIN OR ON YOUR SHORTS?

"I talk to so many people about this," Mathews says. "About half the people are like me, and put it in their shorts. I put it on the pad, fold the pad over, smear it around, then put the shorts on. That works great for me. The other half want to put it on their skin, and that works great too. But it all ends up in the same place, so it's whatever works for you."

If you only have a few small areas that are having issues with friction and are ending up chafed post-ride, you might be better off applying directly to those spots, to make sure you get chamois cream where it's the most needed.

HOW MUCH DO I USE?

It doesn't take much. "Our small packets are 9ml and most people use between half and all of that," says Mathews. "If it's squishing around, coming out of your shorts, you're using too much." The optimal amount is about a quarter-size, a bit more if you have a lot of chafing spots.

WHAT SEPARATES CHAMOIS CREAM FROM A DIAPER RASH OINTMENT?

"A lot of diaper rash ointments have zinc oxide in them," Mathews explains. "That's actually a drying agent. It's a friction producer, so if you use that, you get more friction." Note: If you forget chamois cream and end up with some angry chafing down there, that's when you may want to have some diaper rash ointment hanging around! Consider it a post-ride solution rather than an in-ride problem solver.

WHAT'S THE DIFFERENCE WITH WOMEN'S CHAMOIS CREAMS?

"We've always made our products so that men and women could both use them," Mathews explains. "We did a lot of research though, and the thing that we came up with was that the difference between men's and women's skin, and the perineal area, was that women's skin has a lower pH. It's more acidic. Most women don't have major problems with a minor change in pH. But some women are exceptionally sensitive to changes in pH, and if they get a product introduced to that area that changes their pH, it can throw it off, they can get yeast infections, and they have all kinds of problems."

This isn't all women, of course, but some women are sensitive. If you suspect you might be one of them, there are a few chamois creams that boast pH-balancing properties. In Chamois Butt'r Her', Mathews says, "We lowered the pH for a woman, so it's less likely to throw someone's pH off. And that's what we've heard: women who are really sensitive are saying that they have much fewer problems."

He added, "We also wanted some naturally occurring antibacterial products for this cream, and we get that with lavender and tea tree oil. Both are milder than the menthol in Eurostyle."

Reader Question:
Keeping it Natural?

Is it OK to put something like coconut oil as a lubricant-barrier, plus padded biking underwear, plus a pair of padded biking shorts to prevent too much rubbing? I have a constant pain problem so I also apply freezing gel called xylacaine.

First of all, ouch! I think what you might be suffering from is actually too much friction-fighting gear. If I were in your position, I would:

1) Take a few days off the bike and let any chafing heal. Keep your lady parts as cool and dry as possible, and use something like Neosporin for any raw skin (the time off to heal is the hardest, but it's important!)

2) When you do get back, I'd opt for just one chamois, versus two, and I love a chamois cream designed for women and with some antimicrobial properties. I think part of your problem right now is the combination of stuff you're using is actually creating more and more sliding since now you're a bit over-lubricated, plus you have two chamois pushing against each other, and with the numbing cream, you may not be noticing it in-ride. I'd personally avoid the coconut oil in this case (though it's a fabulous post-ride moisturizer—I use it on my legs all the time!).

3) Consider a bike fit if you haven't had one—you might have your saddle a bit too high or too low and that might be contributing to friction. And if you've already done that, I'd consider swapping saddles—get measured at a local shop (they can find the width of your sit bones) so you get a saddle sized right for you, and opt for one with a bit of padding, but not a ton. A lot of times, the cushy saddles lead to the worst chafing: your pelvic bones are constantly pushing down looking for stability and the foam gets in the way!

SENSITIVITY AND THE SADDLE

"Always watch out for pain: if you have any pain while you're riding, clitoral pain, vaginal pain, pelvic pain, butt pain—that's pressure that might lead to problems." That's what Gynecologist Kristi Angevine advises the women she works with. An ounce of prevention is worth a pound of cure… And can help you skip some nasty saddle issues!

Let's start with a slightly terrifying set of facts. A study done in 2005 and published in the *European Urology Journal* begins, "Bicycle riding is one of the most popular means of transportation, recreation, fitness and sports among millions of people of all ages who ride on road and off road, using a variety of bicycle types."

OK, that's not super scary. Actually, it's pretty rad. This is where it gets bad: "Bicycles are also a common source of significant injuries. This review focuses upon the specific bicycling related overuse injuries affecting the genitourinary tract."

The results? Not awesome for those of us who love to ride a lot.

"The reported incidence of bicycling related urogenital symptoms varies considerably. The most common bicycling associated urogenital problems are nerve entrapment syndromes presenting as genitalia numbness, which is reported in 50–91% of the cyclists, followed by erectile dysfunction reported in 13–24%."

50-91 percent of cyclists are reporting numbness? This seems problematic. (And we'll touch on the erectile dysfunction later, but suffice to say: yikes.) But, if that's the case, what can we do to alleviate this issue?

First of all, don't panic if you are one of the people who suffers from the occasionally numb nether regions. It's preventable and avoidable. To start with, refer to the past chapters. Get a saddle that makes you comfortable, a bike fit, and a pair of shorts that makes you comfortable. But as we all know, nothing is ever going to make cycling feel perfect. There's always going to be some issue—but what can make or break your cycling career is whether you accept the discomfort, or take a solution-focused approach.

HOW DO I KEEP FROM GOING NUMB IN THE SADDLE?

In short? You can change the way you ride and how your ride feels with one minor movement: Standing. "I try to take a skill bias with any athlete, meaning I start with the skill component, then add some intensity, then add volume, versus the traditional 'Let's go ride our bike for 50 hours and try to do an Ironman,'" says longtime coach Peter Glassford. "To that end, we can play with saddles and play with bike fit, but there are a lot of skills we forget too often, and the first one would be the skill of standing while riding. This isn't a female-specific thing, but until you get to really talented athletes, the idea of standing up is so discouraged for efficiency, or because it's associated with sprinting. But you can and should stand for four pedal strokes, let some pressure off, readjust, and sit back down. And it makes a huge difference."

'Yes, a saddle that doesn't fit well won't feel great, but I think you can let off a lot of that pressure by these little periodic standing breaks," he continues. "What I see is that a lot of people who really struggle to the point of not being able to ride with saddle sores are the people who stand up poorly or not at all. So what I encourage is just starting to stand more. Not on a spin bike, not on a trainer, but outside on an actual bicycle, getting the bike moving from side to side. It's going to let you use that standing posture, which will make you faster all around, and it makes the fit of your bicycle less important, so the comfort should be increased. I think standing is something you never see talked about, but it's greatly going to affect your comfort and performance. Taking your butt off the saddle is going to feel good, and doing it efficiently is going to make you faster."

Marketing VP and Creative Director at Terry Bicycles, Paula Dyba, echoes Glassford's sentiment. "New riders often won't stand up or move, and their saddles tend to be too low." That's where adjusting fit comes in. "That's the number one concern: saddles being too low for new riders. That hurts everything."

On that note, Heidi Grissom Bell, MD, says that studies have shown that a less aggressive riding position, in which handlebars are above the level of your bike seat, can help alleviate some numbing problems caused by too much weight being pressed on your nether regions as you bend over to hold onto the bars.

POST-RIDE, MY NETHER REGIONS ARE SUPER SENSITIVE FOR A WHILE, ESPECIALLY AFTER A RACE. IS THERE ANY WAY I CAN ALLEVIATE THIS?

"This is very normal for women," says gynecologist and cyclist Kristi Angevine. "The labia, clitoris, clitoral hood, and vaginal area can be sensitive after any riding, but especially so after a hard effort at a race. This is because in a race, we may stay in a particular position or be moving frequently and aggressively from one position to another without paying much attention to comfort because of our focus on the competition itself. When possible, making sure you aren't in the same saddle position for a prolonged period of time can help. Intermittently, make small adjustments to your position or briefly stand up to relieve pressure. Other than making sure you ride with a clean, comfortable chamois with chamois cream on a saddle that suits you, there's not much to do about it besides realize this post-ride sensitivity is normal and transient. If the problems intensifies or becomes severe, consult a doctor."

To simplify that even further, gynecologist Esther Yun says, "Sensitivity in the genital area is usually due to pressure and irritation. Check that your bike, saddle, and chamois fit you well. Shift your weight frequently during your ride to distribute pressure and give your lady parts a break."

Boom.

BUT IT STILL HURTS. WHAT ELSE CAN I DO?

If you are sore after a ride, you can apply a cool compress (like a cool towel... not ice!) explains Yun. "This will decrease any swelling of the labia as well as provide some pain relief. If you're brave, you can do a sitz bath with some cool—no cold!—water."

Still sore the next day? Opt for warm (not hot!) water baths—"a few inches of clean, warm water in a clean tub," according to Yun—two or three times daily for just 10 to 15 minutes. "This will soothe the irritated skin and promote healing by promoting blood flow. If you have just raced, hopefully you have a day or two that you can go for easier, shorter rides or take a rest day."

And if it still hurts after a few days, take it to the experts. "Consider paying a visit to your friendly neighborhood gynecologist if you have persistent pain, whether you're riding 5 miles a week or 500," says Yun, because your pain may not be from cycling alone.

What if I can't take it easy?

"If you are racing again, continue the cool compresses until you're through racing—until you are no longer causing irritation or injury to the tissue—and then follow the same directions," says Yun. "If you have persistent pain, you are either in the middle of riding the Tour Divide or another crazy endurance race—Holy cow! I'm impressed... and jealous!—or there's something does not fit right on your bike or in your shorts." That means going back to the first few chapters and working on saddle choice, chamois choice, and bike fit.

But for fast relief, right now, the best cool compress advice comes from Jade Wilcoxson, 2013 Road National Champion. "Men are sitting on smooth skin. We're sitting on folds," she says. "Men should ride in wrinkly jeans to get the same effect! What I started doing at track camp, I went out and bought one of those gel eye masks that you freeze. It's a good shape if you find one without the eye-holes. You can also disinfect it! I had a 40-minute commute to the track in LA, so I'd take the eye mask to the track in an icebox, then stuff it in my pants and ice on the way home."

Sounds crazy, but it's a weirdly elegant solution.

I keep getting yeast infections. Is it from riding?

Maybe. "I've seen issues with yeast infections," says shop worker Samantha Stumpf. "Usually it happens when women wear cheaper shorts, or women wear underwear, so it's more of a hygiene situation combined with doing longer rides." [See the section on Keeping It Clean for more details.]

After rides and races, especially cyclocross ones, I've had a lot of problems with swelling. It lasts for a week or so. Am I potentially causing long-term damage?

First of all, don't panic. "Swelling of the labia minora and majora—the inner, delicate labial lips and the outer, more fleshy skin—can be a common issue related to the ever-present problem of friction when riding," says Angevine. And cyclocross—that hard, short effort that forces you on and off the bike in a less-than-optimal manner—can make friction worse. Not to mention, we tend to skip cool downs post-race, or hang out in our chamois just a little too long after races while chatting with friends.

"Most typically, labial swelling from friction is related to a few things: a saddle that rubs, a poor bike position or fit, a chamois that is too thick or too thin, lack of chamois cream, or being in one prolonged position," she adds. "If swelling is transient and seems to just occur with rides, it is most likely nothing dangerous. However, not all labial swelling is benign: infection, impaired lymphatic drainage and other problems can manifest as swelling, so seeing a health care provider familiar with this issue could be important."

EVEN HOURS AFTER A RIDE, I'VE BEEN EXPERIENCING A LOT OF ITCHINESS AND VAGINAL DRYNESS. IS THERE SOME WAY I CAN PREVENT IT?

Don't assume that cycling is the problem: you might be dealing with hormonal issues or complications from medication. "Itchiness and dryness during or after rides is tricky," says Angevine. "Like many irritating vulvar issues, itchiness can be related to friction, improper bike or saddle fit, or more serious problems. Itch in particular can be related to bacteria or yeast infections or to dermatological problems."

For bike-oriented switches, consider switching chamois creams if the one you typically use isn't working. If you're riding long, even consider bringing a small amount of cream with you to reapply during the ride, but, of course, make sure you're getting clean quickly post-ride.

Often, this problem is cited by older riders who are nearing or in menopause, and the fluctuation in hormones is partially to blame.

If it truly is happening after every ride, Angevine says you should talk to your gynecologist. "Dryness can be related to cycling itself, to menopause, to stress, to medications we take and to a variety of other factors," she adds. "The same rules usually apply for both of these issues—if you minimize friction and get clean immediately after a ride and are still having problems, you need to see a doctor." (Also see the chapter on Menopause later in this book.)

READER QUESTION: UTIs?

I keep getting urinary tract infections, and I noticed that they occur around big training blocks. Are the two connected?

"The female urethra is very short compared to the urethra of a male, so bacteria in our cycling shorts can move into our bladder easily and set up camp," explains Angevine. "Urinating flushes this bacteria out; removing the chamois and cleaning off reduces the bacteria that could move in. Sometimes, recurrent UTIs are managed with a preventative antibiotic, so talking with your physician could be key to minimizing this issue."

Lia Sonnenburg, a Doctor of Naturopathic Medicine, adds that riding your bike is always going to exacerbate an existing issue. "If you're post-menopausal and not producing enough estrogen, the tone in the bladder changes and you're more prone to infections, so that saddle time is making it more inflamed, leading to more UTIs. And then it's a cyclical thing, and to break the cycle, you may need to take a broader view of health and not just focus on the bike part."

"Recurrent urinary tract infections—UTIs—are a huge annoyance for anyone. The first step in managing them is to confirm the diagnosis with a urine test," says Angevine.

"There are several other things that can masquerade as a UTI and ensuring you are treating the correct culprit will save time and hassle. If recurrent UTI is indeed the issue, make sure that riding is the only variable that seems to affect their frequency since some folks have UTIs related to increased sexual activity."

This is actually great advice across the board, if you're having feminine 'issues.' Keep a log of your training, your cycle, and how you're feeling each day and any problems you have. That way, you and your coach, or you and your doctor, can look for common patterns to find a solution. If nothing jumps out, add more data, like a food log, or even a log of any sexy time or time spent in public pools or hot tubs, since, as Angevine pointed out, there are other causes of UTIs.

You can do the following to help prevent them in the future:

1. Urinate frequently—before and during rides (but not in your chamois!)

2. Right after you ride, change out of your chamois and clean off with water or a baby wipe if you can't shower soon (while waiting for the podium, of course).

3. A homeopathic cure for constant UTIs is drinking cranberry juice because of the high Vitamin C content (and the alternative is simply taking more Vitamin C). It's not a doctor-approved cure, but if you're having some problems with what seems to be a low-level UTI, consider up-ing your Vitamin C in the form of fruits and just a plain vitamin. Worst case, you're taking in a few extra nutrients.

That said, don't mess with UTIs. They seem like a minor annoyance at first, but if left untreated, they can lead to much worse full-body infections, so consult a doctor if it's a recurring problem, or won't go away.

YOUR PELVIC FLOOR & YOU

One of the most frequently ignored muscles in the body is the pelvic floor—it's hard to work out, impossible to see, and until you actually have a problem, it can be difficult to comprehend the importance of taking care of it. So, to find out why it's so important and what you can do to keep your pelvic floor in tip-top shape, I talked to Laura Powers (BPHE, MPT), a physiotherapist in Collingwood, Ontario. She's been focusing on helping women—primarily athletes—correct their pelvic floors for the past few years, and considers educating the public on the topic to be one of her primary passions.

Why does the pelvic floor matter?

It's a major muscle, just like any other! We'll get into the problems women can have with their pelvic floor, but those problems, when left unaddressed, can really affect everyday life: your self esteem, your social life, your confidence, what you enjoy doing… We can help women so much.

What are the most common pelvic floor issues you see in female cyclists?

One in four women have some kind of urinary incontinence, so if you take athletes and apply that to them, it's not as uncommon as you might think. For cyclists in particular, though, it's a low impact sport with no jumping, so stress urinary incontinence isn't as common. Most commonly, I'm seeing women with pelvic pain, numbness, sexual dysfunction—they just can't get orgasms—all due to the prolonged compression on the saddle. There are a lot of nerves, veins and arteries that get compressed and can create those sensations. That's likely what we see: deeper, inside pelvic pain, superficial numbness, or that sexual dysfunction. If you're avoiding sex because of discomfort, that's a bad sign.

What are some early warning signs that a woman needs to do something about her pelvic floor?

As a female athlete, if you've had a baby, you should be doing pelvic floor exercises or seeking preventative treatment. I advocate for seeking some kind of guidance after childbirth. But in terms of early signs, those symptoms I mentioned in the last question often start out infrequently or in more mild forms. If it goes unaddressed, it gets worse. Pain becomes longer and more intense. So any of those symptoms are signs that something isn't right: even a little bit of leakage isn't normal. A bit of discomfort on the saddle isn't abnormal, but if you're having it, you should think about ways to make your ride more comfortable to avoid the issues getting worse.

What certifications should a cyclist look for when looking for someone to help?

A lot of physiotherapists claim to treat pelvic floor, but a lot of them only do external work. They'll educate on positioning and how to engage your core, and that's fabulous and greatly needed. But you probably want someone who does internal exams and assessment, who will internally palpate the muscles. That makes a big difference. When looking for one, look for a physiotherapist registered to do internal palpations for the pelvic floor. It's the most effective way to assess and treat pelvic floor problems. Women come in all the time and tell me they've been doing Kegels, and I do an exam and it doesn't feel like they've done anything because they haven't been doing them properly. And what we need to assess is the tightness of the pelvic floor. There's a certain tightness that's considered healthy. In a weak pelvic floor, the muscles feel softer and that's when you tend to have that stress incontinence. On the other hand, a high-tone pelvic floor feels tight and restricted. That's when you see more pelvic pain issues. Both require very, very different treatments, and that gets missed with external treatments.

What can a patient expect going for the internal treatment?

It's similar to when you go for a physical. But when women think of that, you think of the speculum and having your feet in the stirrups. But it's not like that. You'll feel some pressure, but most women say it's not as bad or as weird as they thought it would be! It's not very invasive, and it's a comfortable setting. But people are nervous about the internal part—I just tell people they're in complete control and we can stop anytime.

What are some exercises a woman can do to strengthen pelvic floor?

I'm a huge proponent of home exercises because I only see women once a week. They need to be doing home exercise to maintain the work that we're doing. For a cyclist with a tight pelvic floor, that means lots of stretches. I like Child's Pose, deep breathing, anything to create relaxation. If you have loose muscles though, that's when we're doing Kegels. But really, it's like any other training program— just like other muscles, they need that training effect. You'd go for regular massages and stretch if you had tight neck muscles!

If you're wondering about your pelvic floor during and after pregnancy, make sure to check out those chapters for Laura's takes on those topics. And visit ConsummateAthlete.com for the full podcast with Laura discussing the pelvic floor and athletes.

POST-RIDE CARE

The best defense is a good offense, and in this case, the best way to treat a saddle sore is to avoid it altogether. And that means taking care of proper bike fit, saddle and shorts choice, and proper application of chamois cream. But it also means that you need to practice perfect post-ride hygiene.

"After a long ride, the best thing you can do is get out of those biking clothes as soon as possible," says gynecologist Esther Yun. "If there is any skin damage, you want to decrease the amount of time that skin is in contact with your sweaty chamois—less rubbing—and get it clean and dry quickly."

In fact, this is particularly important for sensitive women. "If you are prone to vaginal irritation or infections, this is particularly important. If you're sensitive, absolutely don't drive home in that soggy chamois," says gynecologist Kristi Angevine.

If possible, jump in the shower and spray down that area immediately, and carefully. A lot of us tend to skimp on attention paid to our nether regions in the shower, but make sure you get those nooks and crannies (especially spots like where your butt cheeks meet your thigh) extra clean. If there is skin damage, both Yun and naturopath Lia Sonnenburg recommend that you can consider a sitz bath or an epsom salt bath to decrease inflammation and soothe the irritated tissues.

Almost as important as washing carefully is making sure to fully dry your under-carriage post-shower. "Let the area dry completely after bathing," says Yun. "Try not to rub it with a towel; I often suggest women use a hair dryer on cool to dry more sensitive areas if there is any irritation." Sonnenburg also recommends this.

Skip the harsh rubbing with an old towel: that can irritate the already angry tissue more and, Yun says, if the towel is not fresh, it can seed the area with bacteria and get an infection started.

Not near a shower? Angevine says that you can still get cleaner than you think: just drop your shorts as soon as the ride is over, and travel with wipes. "Use something like a baby diaper wipe or towelette, or even just rinse with some water," she says. Keeping (natural, unscented) baby wipes in your ride-bag is a smart move—and helps you go from mud-covered to office-ready if you sneak in a lunch ride.

"But keep in mind, don't douche or use perfumed spritzers," she adds. "Plain soap and water are all this area needs. Perfumes or douches can alter the pH of the vagina and disrupt the typical balance of the natural vaginal flora. This imbalance leads to vaginitis, bad smelling discharge and itching."

Another great post-ride tip is to try to pee (while you're getting out of that chamois!). If you've been hydrating enough, this shouldn't be an issue, and it might actually keep you from developing UTIs or yeast infections. Heidi Grissom Bell, MD, says, "Changing in to well-aerated and breathable clothing as soon as possible after your workout will help prevent chronic yeast infections or vaginal pH changes that could lead to bacterial vaginosis. Also, urination after riding helps prevent UTIs—as does wiping 'front-to-back' in any situation!"

In that same vein, Yun notes that it's incredibly important to change out a tampon or Diva Cup post-ride.

Lastly, pay attention to your nether regions after a ride: If you can catch a skin issue early, you'll be at less risk of developing an infection or letting a saddle sore get so out of hand that you need a few days off the bike. "If you notice saddle sores or any other irritation, address it nice and early to prevent future problems," Yun says.

Are you noticing a trend in this chapter? Time to give up that habit of stopping by the coffeeshop on the way home from a long ride and lingering in your bike shorts. Change first, then hang out. Pro tip: I sometimes ride with a spare pair of shorts in my jersey pocket for when I make stops longer than a few minutes— even changing into a pair of running shorts so you're out of your wet chamois while sitting in a coffee shop and then putting the chamois back on is better than sitting in it the whole time.

Saddle Sores

So, you did all of the proper post-ride care, found the best saddle, and still ended up with some serious discomfort. That's a bummer, but we can fix it!

How do I know if I have a saddle sore?

A saddle sore will look and feel like a pimple—a mound that hurts a bit if you press on it. "It may seem similar to an ingrown hair," explains coach Peter Glassford.

Obviously, you'll notice this in the "saddle contact area," most often between your genitalia and your anus. "You'll be more likely to get rashes or simple breakouts on your thighs or butt cheeks," Glassford notes. "Saddle sores are from really abusing the tissue while riding and bacteria gets in there, and the best way to describe it is a big pimple."

But not every little bump "down there" is a saddle sore.

A few of the other common issues include:

1. Ingrown hairs: Between the irritation of wearing tight-fitting, sweaty spandex and shaving (or waxing), ingrown hairs are a distinct possibility and may present similarly to a saddle sore. Treatment for this one is similar though, so even if you treat it the same way, it will heal.

2. Acne: You've likely dealt with acne on your face, but unfortunately, it can be even worse on your butt, and ultimately a saddle sore is just a really big pimple, but smaller breakouts are possible. For this, try an over-the-counter acne cream at

night, and sleep either in the buff or in cotton panties to allow for a good amount of air flow.

3. Jock itch: Not just for guys anymore, unfortunately. This fungal infection (think athlete's foot for your nether regions) presents in a few ways, and usually in a larger area than a single saddle sore would be. Visually, jock itch can range from dry, red, scaly skin to a whole lot of painful small bumps. It will usually be in "fold" areas, so if you have a rash right where your butt cheek meets your thigh, it might be jock itch, not just a pesky rash. Again, there are over-the-counter anti-fungals, but if the two-week treatment doesn't clear it up, check with your doctor.

4. An allergy-induced rash: Maybe you're allergic to your chamois cream, maybe you aren't rinsing your shorts well enough after washing, or maybe you just need a few days off the bike. The best thing to do for a rash—before taking more extreme measures—is to take a cool shower, wash carefully, and give it some time to let it breath before assuming the worst. And double rinse your chamois next time you wash it!

5. Hives: You may have an allergy to something in your chamois, or just a weird allergic reaction in general. An anti-histamine should calm this down, but work on switching detergents or your chamois/chamois cream to see if you can keep it from happening again.

6. Friction rash: "A friction rash is more often on the thighs or buttocks and might remind you of a sunburn or heat rash: There won't be much tactile difference as far as bumps, just the stinging discomfort of a rash," says Glassford. "These are going to need different treatment then a saddle sore might need, and generally adding some medicated lotion will help."

Of course, to prevent all of these issues, check out the chapters on proper chamois and saddle fit, as well as the one on post-ride care. And since most of them can be treated like a saddle sore, read on!

How can I keep a saddle sore from getting worse?

Your best bet is to catch it at the onset, rather than waiting for it to get truly big and painful. "Doing a Daily Check is a great way to prevent a major sore," says Glassford. "The first thing you should do is shower when you get off the bike, and do an inspection. See when things are starting to get red or starting to get swollen."

The best way to prevent one from getting worse is to take a day off the bike, ind keep the area as dry and clean as possible. Most of the time, that should be enough to bring the swelling down and let it drain. "If you are insistent on riding, and you are just starting to notice a sore, you can try switching out your chamois, cross-training, changing the type of bike and/or changing your chamois creme strategy—these are all good ways to give that specific section of tissue a break," adds Glassford.

How can I prevent saddle sores?

"Doctors and gynecologists will give you all these medications, but it's so rare that one warns you to just take off your shorts faster, clean up, the basic stuff," says Lisa Wilkes, head of customer service at Terry Bicycles. And she's right: often, we ignore the prevention and focus on a cure. Luckily, the gynecologists in this book are all about avoiding a problem before it starts.

"Saddle sores are not only very uncomfortable, but can turn into a very serious medical issue if not properly addressed early in the process," says gynecologist Esther Yun. So before we worry about how to treat one, let's talk about some prevention methods.

"First off, equipment is important. Your bike should fit you properly. If you're not sure about this, you may want to visit your LBS [local bike shop] for a fitting," says Yun.

"Having your weight balanced in the wrong way can predispose you to poor riding position and undue weight on the saddle as a result," she adds. "Your saddle should be appropriate both for your pelvis as well as type of activity in order to decrease pressure/chaffing to the buttocks."

You should, of course, have a comfortable chamois. "Always start your ride with a clean, dry chamois," says Yun. "Some people use chamois creams to help with chaffing and as a protectant to help prevent damage to the skin. You may want to consider this if you have very sensitive or delicate skin."

And remember that you are adding another skin product, so beware of allergies/sensitivities as well. Avoid products with perfumes, dyes, or large amounts of preservatives.

"Changing positions on the saddle and standing during your ride will also help prevent sores, as it redistributes and relieves pressure," she adds.

Echoing that, Glassford says that there isn't one simple fix: Your body is a series of systems. "I think if we empower athletes with the ability to slightly tweak their setup, to do things like altering saddle height by a couple millimeters to get a better feel on a day after travel or after stretching for a month, then we can greatly reduce discomfort, maximize performance, and have more fun."

WHAT DOES GETTING A SADDLE SORE MEAN FOR MY RIDING?

"First of all, you should look at a saddle sore as a limiter: Think of it as a way of your body telling you you're going too far and need to recover," says Glassford. "If you're struggling with saddle sores, a big thing to do is to make a change. I take it as a sign that your body isn't adapting, like any other sign of overtraining. Usually I'll just take a day off. I think people aren't quick to do that, but I just treat it like any other limiter, whether you're sore muscularly or you have a bad cough."

"I think taking a break is the hardest thing to do when it's just a saddle sore and it's not your legs, but it's important," he adds.

It might also mean that your bike fit isn't right. And that's a hard pill to swallow, especially if we've previously had a bike fit. "We are so hesitant to make changes to our bikes, especially if it's a bike fit from the shop or some super pro bike fitter. But making a change, whether it's dropping the seat height, changing the saddle, moving the saddle forward—tinkering away with it, can help," Glassford believes. "I think this idea of tinkering is under-utilized. Making changes and taking control of the situation is something I rarely see. I don't think bike fit is this mysterious thing that we've made it out to be, which is a fairly controversial view. I just don't believe that if you have decent mobility, every day you need to be within this one millimeter of perfection."

So take responsibility for your own perfect fit: The experts aren't always right, especially if you don't tell them about your particular lady part problems with regards to the bike. A fitter is trying to make you efficient on the bike, not necessarily correcting for comfort in the nether regions. "By enabling the athlete to make changes when they're having an issue with fit, we can improve the situation," Glassford says. "Does the saddle sore hurt less if you move the seat up, down, forward, backward? That should be a pretty good indicator, and it's something you can do with this day off that we're talking about. You can do that in your driveway."

WHAT SHOULD I DO ABOUT A SADDLE SORE?

"Saddle sores start when friction breaks the surface of the skin enough for bacteria that normally lives on our skin's surface to get underneath. This defect plus bacteria forms a sore that can be difficult to care for given its location," explains gynecologist Kristi Angevine.

If you catch it early, keep treatment simple: Clean and dry. "The worst thing to do is squeeze. It crushes the tissue around it and pisses it off," says Matt Marchal, a family practitioner, team doctor and long-time rider. "There's no magic fix for a saddle sore. Address it as soon as you notice it. It's like a leak in your roof: If you catch it as soon as you find it, it'll normalize pretty quickly. But if you let it go, you might end up with a huge mess."

"Epsom salt baths are great," says Lia Sonnenburg, a Doctor of Naturopathic Medicine. "I'm very generous with the salt I put in the baths—4 to 6 cups of epsom salt in a bath!"

She also recommends clients try a more natural remedy of a bit of tea tree oil with coconut oil, after you've cleaned and dried the area. "I recommend drying your nether regions with a hair dryer—not too close—to dry off without rubbing down with a towel."

If it's starting to hurt, Glassford adds, "I've always been big on tea tree oil. Just something antiseptic and soothing. If I start getting issues, I use something like Neosporin, or any antibiotic ointment." Just note that tea tree oil should be from a pure, reputable source versus buying a cheap blend, and test it on a patch of skin on which you can afford to have an allergic reaction prior to applying directly to that more sensitive skin.

WHEN SHOULD I SEE A DOCTOR?

As Angevine said, if you develop a fever, or the skin around the saddle sore is red, inflamed, and painful, it might be time for medical intervention.

If it hasn't gone away in a couple of days, that's another reason to make an appointment. "It is possible you have developed an infection, such as an abscess, or caused such extensive damage that the fat and/or muscle tissue has broken down, much like bed sores in the ill," says Yun. "If this is the case, you should consult your physician for evaluation and treatment."

A doctor can prescribe antibiotics for potential infections, and might even be able to drain a particularly bad saddle sore.

WHAT WILL A DOCTOR DO FOR ME?

First of all, Marchal warns of doctors who immediately prescribe antibiotics without looking at the sore to consider draining it. "If you don't take care of cyclists, you're not familiar with a saddle sore, so a lot of doctors just prescribe antibiotics. And sometimes, that's fine," he says. "But if the saddle sore is bad enough, it might need to be opened up and drained so the bad stuff can get out, and so those two layers of skin that are separated can stick back together. So antibiotics without draining it, especially if you keep riding, might mean it'll heal partially, but it could keep coming back. And if that happens enough, you may need surgery because you'll have a buildup of scar tissue there too."

Worst case scenario? "I've seen a racer end up in the hospital because of an infected saddle sore," Marchal recalls. "The infection got in his bloodstream and he ended up with sepsis. So the worst case scenario is that you can get super sick from these things if you try to push through."

And that's why you shouldn't wait to see a doctor if your saddle sore has been lingering or if you're getting feverish: better to be off the bike for a week than a full season. "If you come to me early, it could be gone, as opposed to coming to me after it's gotten bad and we now need an emergency plan," he adds.

WHAT ABOUT THOSE INGROWN HAIRS?

"If you notice little bumps, they are likely due to ingrown hairs or clogged pores," explains gynecologist Esther Yun. The best way to treat them is to use a warm, moist compress.

"You can use a washcloth soaked in clean, warm water or nuke a moist cloth for 20-30 seconds," Yun says, but adds that if you choose to nuke it, make sure it is not too hot before applying it. "No one wants a scalded and saddle-sore bum!"

Make sure you use a fresh washcloth each time—you can do this every few hours, depending on how sore you are, until said bump comes to a head and drains, or it settles down.

If it is an ingrown hair, do not dig around and try to pluck it! Yun says that plucking is an invitation for it to be a new ingrown hair next week. "Let's not invite trouble," she says. "Let the hair come above the skin surface and let the skin heal completely before shaving/ waxing/removing."

MY SKIN IS CHAFED: WHAT SHOULD I DO?

If your saddle sore is more chafed or broken skin, you can still use the warm water or epsom salt baths for comfort, says Yun, but you should keep the skin as dry as possible.

"Consider sleeping without underwear to allow the skin to breathe and heal," she adds. "Spend as much time in loose, breathable clothing (or naked!) as you can. If possible, consider taking a few days off or easy to let the skin heal."

"I see chafed skin very often. It's a similar protocol to saddle sores—keep the area dry, use the blow dryer after the shower to make sure it's dry, and then use a medical grade Manuka honey with an old pair of underwear because it's really sticky," says Sonnenburg. "If you can do that twice a day, that's great... I use it on my pregnant women because it really helps with perineal tearing during labor, but cyclists keep coming to the clinic and buying all of mine!"

And, of course, Yun and Sonnenburg both recommend using a protectant when you are riding until the skin has healed. And remember to get out of those sweaty shorts, showered, and dry as soon as possible after each ride!

LAST WORDS

The best thing that you can ultimately do is to keep an eye out for these issues, and catch them early. The worst thing you can do is to continue to train and ride as usual without treating them, since saddle sores can quickly go from bad to worse—there have been cases of ruined season, surgeries, and permanent disfigurement and discomfort.

YOUR QUICK GUIDE TO SADDLE SORE TREATMENT

If you grabbed this book just to figure out what the heck to do about a terrible saddle sore, here are your quick tips from gynecologist Kristi Angevine.

When off the bike, keep it clean and dry. Wash it with plain soap and water.

Let the area breathe by avoiding underwear made of satin or silk. Opt for cotton, wool, any breathable fabrics, or no underwear at all.

Warm baths and hot compresses can be soothing.

Don't squeeze it! That prolongs healing and increases the chances of a larger infection.

If it gets really irritated, or is very painful when riding, take a few days off the saddle.

For general perineal and vaginal health, and not just when there is a saddle sore: Wear only clean shorts, not ones that have been worn on a ride before and haven't been washed. Also, after doing any exercise, change out of your workout clothing and get clean soon. This means get out of that chamois before you drive home!

See a doctor if the skin around the area gets red, hot, or swollen, or if you get a fever.

KEEPING IT CLEAN

One question I've heard over and over comes back to post-ride care, and care in general. How should I keep my lady parts clean? Thanks to the ever-growing beauty industry, we're bombarded by products for feminine hygiene that are packed with chemicals and scents and dyes. But really, what you need is a bar of good, old-fashioned soap.

"Nature was good enough to make us 'self-cleansing' for the most part," explains gynecologist Esther Yun. "The more we mess with things, the worse they tend to get. Your body has a natural pH balance as well as bacterial balance that keeps everything in check. All you have to do is prevent this balance from being disrupted."

And that means that the vagina does not need to be cleaned. "The natural mucous produced by the cervix is designed to keep your pH balance in check and push out foreign substances," says Yun. That means you should shy away from things like douches. "Avoid douching at all costs—we want to avoid our pesky enemy, pelvic inflammatory disease (PID)! Douching can also cause problems with infection by pushing bacteria from the vagina and genital area into the otherwise sterile uterus."

"The labia minora—non hair-bearing areas—can be cleaned with a mild soap, such as Dove or Aveeno white bars, and warm water. Avoid any products with antibacterial or antibiotic properties, perfumes, dyes, and deodorants—this applies to feminine hygiene products as well," Yun says.

In general, Yun says to avoid things labeled as "feminine cleansing" products, including wipes, gels, washes, and special soaps. "You are more likely to throw your body off balance by adding things to the mix."

The caveat, of course, is if you are experiencing irritation, odor, or pain. In that case, Yun says, consult your doctor immediately. "Your doctor may suggest specific products to help you maintain a good pH balance and help prevent irritation," she adds, but don't self-diagnose.

But really, what it comes down to, is that post-ride care: Take Off Your Shorts. "The best thing you can do for yourself is to get out of those sweaty clothes and bathe as soon as possible," Yun concludes.

CRAMPS, PERIODS, AND TAMPONS

Being a woman can be tough—especially for that one week during the month when riding becomes a bit more complicated, thanks to our periods. I remember being on one long ride with a group of guys and one other woman. She was in her new, all-white kit. You can probably guess where this story is going.

Naturally, she ended up getting her period mid-ride, in the middle of nowhere. And, of course, I wasn't equipped to help. She ended up riding with one of the guy's windbreakers tied around her waist the rest of the ride, and I have never felt worse for a friend. Since then, I've always ridden with a tampon tucked into my saddlebag, because you never know when you'll need to help a fellow rider out— and that's the kind of help that wins you a new best friend.

But let's talk about periods, cramping, and how you can make your bike ride feel better.

IS IT BETTER TO RIDE WITH A TAMPON OR PAD DURING YOUR PERIOD?

"Like most things having to do with vaginal health, this is a personal choice, and everyone has their own rationale for their menstrual cycle paradigm," says gynecologist Kristi Angevine. "In my opinion, tampons are infinitely easier, because unlike wearing a pad, there is no material to contend with. Pads are fraught with many more challenges because they can bunch up, move out of position, and ultimately rub in ways that cause skin breakdown and irritation."

Remember that bit about why underwear is bad to wear under your shorts? It's the same for pads. "Pads tend to wrinkle and become irritants to the skin over time, especially if pressed closely to the skin by the bike saddle," says Heidi Grissom Bell, MD. "And if pads are used, they should be unscented. Perfumes that are used in scented pads can be really irritating to the skin over time!"

But if you're not comfortable with tampons—or alternatives like the Diva Cup (a small soft rubber cup that is inserted similar to a tampon but collects the blood in the cup and is reusable)—at the end of the day, you should use what you are most comfortable with, says gynecologist Esther Yun.

There are some advantages to using a tampon: In addition to avoiding the chafing and potential wedgie caused by a pad, a tampon will decrease the moisture present in the area. "That decreases irritation to the sensitive skin in the area," says Yun.

"The string should also be tucked in to minimize chafing," she adds. I've heard this issue referred to as "rope burn"—if it's a long string, even consider trimming it slightly, but not to the point where you risk losing it.

With whatever method you use, though, Yun says what's essential is that you change it on a regular basis, especially if you are having a heavy flow day.

"Retained tampons and leaving tampons in for extended periods of time predisposes you to risk of infection, specifically toxic shock syndrome," she adds.

And a pad isn't any better: "Leaving a pad on for extended periods of time, especially during and after exercise, and especially while wearing a chamois, will hold and trap moisture, discharge, and bacteria. This can predispose you to bacterial vaginosis and/or yeast infections," Yun says.

If you suspect you've developed one of these infections, check with a doctor before trying to treat it. "Because both these infections can manifest with similar symptoms, it is important to contact your gynecologist if symptoms persist so that you receive the appropriate treatment," she adds.

Any tricks for dealing with PMS cramps?

Cramping during a ride is, simply put, the worst. During your period, that can ruin an interval or stymy a century like nothing else can. The best thing to do is to plan your rest week in tandem with your period if you know cramping is a problem—or if you work with a coach, make sure he or she is aware that you prefer rest weeks correspond with your cycle—so you have a slightly easier ride schedule to contend with. Outside of that, make sure all other reasons for cramping—dehydration and bonking [where your body starts fatiguing due to lack of sugar], specifically—are under control. I've found that my period can make my stomach clench up as soon as I'm slightly dehydrated, and long before I've normally started to bonk, so I try to think ahead and be prepared for that.

From the medical side, there are a few options as well. "Ooooooh... craaaaamp! And not in the legs! Oh, the joys of the being a woman... As if wrangling with the last question wasn't enough, now you have menstrual cramps to boot! Luckily, modern medicine can really help with this," Yun says.

"If you are on hormonal birth control such as the pill, patch, or ring, you may want to consider talking to your doctor about your options as far as birth control is concerned, she suggests.

"For those who are not using birth control or using other methods, there is still hope! Taking ibuprofen before a ride can also decrease cramping during that ride," Yun adds. "It can, however, thin your blood and make you more prone to bruising/bleeding if you have a fall, so be careful out there! This is not safe for everyone, so please consult your physician before starting such a regimen."

WHAT IF THEY'RE REALLY AWFUL PERIOD CRAMPS?

If you frequently find yourself cramping to the point where you can't ride, certainly seek medical attention. "Dysmenorrhea, or painful periods, can be a huge nuisance while riding," says Angevine. "One of the simplest ways to minimize the discomfort during this time is to take ibuprofen or naproxen in a specific way. Ibuprofen and naproxen block some of the hormones that make the uterus cramp. Taking 600-800mg of ibuprofen every six hours or 500mg of naproxen every 12 hours starting 48 hours before your period, or just as soon as you think it's starting, and through to the end of your cycle can minimize cramps and also cut down on bleeding by about 30 percent."

"The key is to take the medicine before you need it, and to take it routinely. A small amount of caffeine can also help the medicine's pain relieving qualities," she says. "Of course, you should confirm with your physician that taking these medicines in this way is safe for you, because they can cause irritation to the lining of the stomach, as well as exacerbate other medical problems you might have," she adds. And if you're training heavily, make sure your doctor is aware of that when you ask about starting this regimen, because that's a lot of painkillers over time.

Do Your Laundry Right

Just like sensitive skin anywhere else, your nether regions can be particularly reactive to foreign substances. This includes lotions, washes, powders, wipes, soaps, and detergent.

If you have chronic irritation, consider switching all products to hypo-allergenic (no perfumes or dye) alternatives, especially when it comes to laundry products and soaps.

One of the biggest problems I've seen with cyclists who have chronic saddle sores or rashes is that their laundry practices are sloppy. Chamois aren't getting washed fully or rinsed thoroughly, they're being bombarded by harsh scents and dyes, or they're not being completely dried.

So, as it turns out, your laundry habits might be what's causing skin "issues" when you ride. But thankfully, there are a few key habits that you can start to alleviate a whole lot of on-bike problems with minimal fuss.

Turn your shorts inside out when you wash them! This should be self-explanatory, but often gets forgotten. When your chamois isn't facing out, a lot of grossness can get left behind in one wash and rinse cycle. If your shorts are super muddy, rinse them first to get the mud mostly off the outside, but always wash so the chamois gets the most attention.

Use hot water, or at least use warm water! Let's kill bacteria and dissolve more of that grime, please.

Consider a sensitive skin detergent. Personally, I like an unscented, dye-free sensitive skin detergent. Some people don't need it, but I find cheaper detergents tend to make my skin break out. When you're wearing Lycra and sweating and have just shaved your legs, it's already a recipe for disaster. Don't make it worse by adding in perfumed detergent that may still be in your shorts when you start riding.

Speaking of that, double rinse. I love the double rinse cycle. It gets everything a little cleaner and gets rid of any extra soap. It's not the most energy efficient, but if you truly have skin issues, this is a big one. I've seen riders start sweating and have soap bubbles come out of their shorts.

Use the dryer. Some people really hate using the dryer on their shorts, but if you're OK with it (and I personally am), using the dryer is the best way to make sure all of the bacteria that's hanging out in your gross shorts is eradicated.

Go green and hang dry, but make sure you do it where sunlight hits your shorts. "One thing if you can is dry shorts outside in the sunlight, because UV rays have great antibacterial qualities," says Steve Mathews, creator of Chamois Butt'r. "Lay them in the sun if you can."

Avoid dampness. Hang drying in a cold, dark area takes forever and gives bacteria that survived the wash cycle the perfect chance to breed before your next ride. Yikes.

Use chemicals with caution. How do you clean a chamois that's gotten blood on it? Periods happen. Thankfully, your chamois can handle bleach, stain stick, whatever you can throw at it. However, the more caustic the chemicals you're using to clean your shorts, the more important that double rinse cycle at the end is. Don't forget it! And if you're extremely sensitive, I'd recommend using the stain stick, washing as normal, and then re-washing and double rinsing, just to make sure all of the chemicals are gone before you wear the shorts again.

YOUR UPPER HALF

Breast health may not come to mind when you think of cycling, but the right sports bra is just as important for cyclists as it is for runners. Choosing a good sports bra, thankfully, is a lot simpler than choosing a good pair of cycling shorts though. Your primary concern is to find one that doesn't hinder breathing when in your normal cycling position, and one that doesn't get in the way of your bib shorts straps if you opt for bib shorts. Ultimately, it's one of the easier decisions you have to make when it comes to cycling equipment.

For a quick recap: Breasts are essentially just fatty tissue that is held in place by ligaments that go from the skin through fat to muscles underneath the breast. That fatty tissue does best when it's held in place during a workout.

If a woman has large breasts and loses weight through exercise, the fat in the breast tissue may be lost as well, which can lead to the appearance of sagging. This is mainly caused by the "bounce effect" that happens during exercise—not a huge issue for most cyclists, but it can be a factor. And this means... You guessed it! You need a good sports bra.

Sagging won't cause medical issues for your breasts or anything drastic, but it makes things a bit less comfortable. If you're concerned about keeping the girls perky as long as possible, wearing a supportive sports bra is probably a good strategy.

Cycling can go either way. You may be a road rider, in which case, a basic sports bra that holds the girls and feels comfortable is fine. If you're a 'crosser or mountain biker who gets jarred around on the bike a lot, an encapsulation bra (one with cups and compression) might be a better move if the girls are shifting a lot.

"We have bras specifically for cycling—you don't need something high-impact for cycling, just something to wick sweat and keep you comfortable so you can focus on your ride," says Lisa Wilkes, head of customer service at Terry Bicycles.

When you're choosing a sports bra for cycling, you want to find one that doesn't make deep breathing feel difficult—especially since, with cycling, most of the time you simply don't need an ultra-high-impact bra, just one that will keep the girls in place while you pedal.

If you wear a heart rate monitor on your rides, bring that to the store when you're trying on sports bras, since you want to find one that works well with the strap under it.

Beyond fit, choosing the right fabric is key. You want to find one that offers moisture-wicking, especially for cycling, where you'll sweat through the front of a bra pretty fast on hot days—and no one wants boob sweat marks coming through her jersey.

My personal favorite piece of advice comes from the American Council of Exercise, which suggests: "When trying on a bra, jump around and try to mimic as best you can the activity you'll be doing while wearing the bra."

This will let you really get a good sense of whether a particular sports bra will work for you. Also, this will be hilarious.

HORMONES AND THE BIKE

First, the scary: don't panic, but there was a study published in the *Journal of Sexual Medicine* entitled "Genital sensation and sexual function in women bicyclists and runners: Are your feet safer than your seat?" OK, that title is pretty alarming.

We know that men can be negatively affected by too much time in the saddle—erectile dysfunction among cycling men isn't uncommon. That said, as Dr. Matt Marchal jokes, "If you look at cyclists—from recreational to the pros who are hoisting kids up on the podium with them—you can see that the guys spending the most time on the bike are showing off their kids. It's not like there are a bunch of Tour pros who are childless." So clearly, sex as a cyclist isn't an impossibility.

And what about for women?

The aforementioned study has good news and bad news. There is an association between bicycling and decreased genital sensation in competitive women cyclists, the study reads. You can revisit the chapters on sensitivity and the saddle for more on that, but look at the bright side: the study concluded, "Negative effects on sexual function and quality of life were not apparent in our young, healthy premenopausal cohort."

Great news, but what does it mean if we are feeling some negative impacts—not just on sex, but on our social lives as a whole—as a result of our training?

Cycling is something that we do because we love it. It's easy to get caught up in training for competition, or for weight loss, and quickly start thinking that more is better, even if it's at the cost of time spent with loved ones, our other hobbies, or even our sex drives. The thing is, though, that the more cycling negatively impacts your everyday life, the less likely it is that your cycling will improve, anyway. Overtraining doesn't actually lead to better results.

LOW SEX DRIVE

First of all, poor you! Sounds like a lot of brutal training—in some cases, overtraining. "I tend to take more of a health bias than most coaches, even with high performance athletes," says coach Peter Glassford. So for him, that's a warning sign not to be ignored. "Would it be normal to have a lowered sex drive from training? If we were really pushing a block of training, you might see a lot of fatigue, but that should resolve after a night of sleep. But if low energy goes on for several days and is combined with low libido, mood change, and other symptoms of overtraining, that is a sign we have pushed too far and that we need to take immediate action."

From a long-term perspective, you should be enjoying your life. "Do you want to jeopardize the health of that tissue, of that organ?" he asks.

You should also be able to get on your bike and go to work... "And you should be able to get off your bike and be a person," he concludes.

So if you're experiencing a low sex drive that you just can't explain, first, take a couple days off the bike. If your sex drive returns in a couple days, you likely just had a bit of fatigue, but if it doesn't come back right away, that's a sign of a more chronic condition and you're going to want to get to the bottom of it. That means it might be time to check in with your doctor or naturopath: There might be something more than just fatigue working against you.

HORMONAL PROBLEMS

Those issues with low-to-no sex drive can be a sign of something a lot more sinister than just a bit of fatigue: It can be an early warning sign for hormonal imbalances. Doctor Jessica Scotchie, Reproductive Endocrinologist and Infertility Specialist, is double board-certified in reproductive endocrinology and infertility, as well as obstetrics and gynecology, so hormones are her game. She says that it's not shocking for cyclists putting in serious training time to have irregular or absent ovulation, which would, in turn, cause irregular cycles—especially if the body weight and body fat get too low, or if the "high level of training stresses the body enough to make it think that procreation would not be optimal, in which case the hypothalamus and pituitary shut down stimulation to the ovary, ceasing ovulation."

A lack of a period may seem like a good thing in the middle of a training or racing block, but it's actually a signal that something is wrong, and needs correcting.

If your cycle is irregular or absent, Scotchie says to see a doctor. "It is important to check a hormone evaluation for ovarian hormones, thyroid hormones and prolactin level... As well as a pregnancy test to make sure there is not another underlying cause of the irregular cycles," she explains. "Barring another abnormality, if the cause is decreased communication between the pituitary and the ovary—which would be the most common cause among athletes—then the solution is to either promote weight gain, decrease training, or begin hormonal medications to replace what the body is not making."

If the first two options are where you start, it can take months or years for the cycles to normalize, and in some women, Scotchie says that they never fully normalize. If that's the case for you, that's when medical interventions may help. "Fortunately, medical therapies to regulate the cycles are very effective, and medications to help pregnancy if and when desired are also highly effective," she adds. "It is very important that cyclists do something to correct the abnormalities, as there are health risks from irregular cycles and from hormone levels being out of balance or deficient, including risk to bone mineral density and long term cardiovascular health."

So please, please do not let your hormones spin out of control because of your... spinning habit.

READER QUESTION: CYCLISTS AND BIRTH CONTROL

As a cyclist, are there any specific birth control methods that will work better (or worse) for me?

If you're using birth control, or planning to start, talk to your gynecologist about your options and mention the level you're riding at. If you're a weekend warrior, this probably won't be an issue. But if you're serious about training and racing, it's worth noting.

Gynecologist Kristi Angevine says that ultimately, the right decision is whatever is the easiest and simplest for someone. "It's very individualized," she adds. "I find a lot of athletes prefer something longer acting, like one of the intrauterine devices that last a few years. But some people will hate it."

Some women I know swear by the birth control pill as a way to not only avoid getting pregnant, but to regulate their cycles so they can plan racing and training roughly around their menses. For others, birth control pills can cause nasty side effects that are exacerbated by training. The level of hormones in some of the commonly prescribed ones can be rough on some women, and in those cases, sometimes an IUD is a better option because of the lower hormone dose. And an IUD is especially useful for women who travel often for racing, who may find taking pills at the same time every day to be a hassle, especially when time zones are involved.

There's no hard and fast "this is what's best for women racers" method, but you should consider your options carefully and choose something that works with your lifestyle.

So—and I'll repeat this often—talk to your gynecologist and let her (or him) know what your life is like. "It's tough when you go to a gynecologist who has never worked with cyclists before," says pro racer Jade Wilcoxson. And she's right. But if you find yourself in that situation, that may mean that you should seek out a new gynecologist, if you feel as though your current one isn't really listening to you.

YOUR HORMONES, NATURALLY

Hormone health is a tricky subject for anyone, whether you just want to ride stronger, you're considering getting pregnant, you're decidedly *not* trying to get pregnant, or you're just having some weird feelings and want to know what's going on. Lia Sonnenburg, a Doctor of Naturopathic Medicine in Collingwood, Ontario, sat down for an interview to talk about some of the most common issues and the natural and lifestyle-oriented ways that we can get our hormones back in balance.

What are some of the chief complaints that you hear from female athletes?
I find, in general, athletes don't like to complain. But the more I question, the more I find things are going on. The biggest complaint is that something has changed and someone wants to know why it's changed—they have a harder time getting out of bed, they feel moody, performance isn't going as well, or they feel like they're not coping as well as they used to. There are so many things going on in everyone's life, and we have to figure out what's causing what.

For female endurance athletes, what are some of the signs of overtraining that you've seen?
The big piece that people don't discuss is that their immune system is getting worn down and they aren't recovering, so they get things like that 100 day cough. And little stuff just knocks them out and they just can't kick it. There are also nuisance afflictions, like athlete's foot or bacterial vaginosis or yeast infections or hangnails that aren't healing, things that are annoying but not causing huge issues. That's stuff I ask about early on, because it's a good sign of overtraining: Your body doesn't have the ability to deal with those little things.

In that same vein, what are some red flags for hormonal imbalance in active women?
I see a lot female athletes having amenorrhea, or not having regular cycles and

they're really inconsistent, and I find a lot of women don't complain about not getting their cycle! That's a huge red flag, though, because we know there's some kind of imbalance that's preventing things from going the way they should. Other red flags are UTIs and vaginal yeast infections with relative frequency. Personal care plays a piece in that, but there may be a hormonal piece perpetuating it.

If a woman suspects her hormones are imbalanced, what are the first things she should do?
The first thing I like to see in women who are still having a normal cycle is to have them track it: How many days are your cycles, how heavy, how's your mood, how's your cramping, how's your flow... We spend a lot of time talking about the cycle to figure out what's going on. If a woman wants a more aggressive approach, based on her family history and personal health history, we'll talk about intelligent testing—we can test hormones in the blood, but those aren't very accurate because they're fat-soluble and often bound to other molecules, so it doesn't give us a good overall picture of what's going on in the body. Saliva and urine testing are better options and give us a lot more useful information. That gives us an idea of how well you're balanced.

How do you know what's low?
It's hard to know. We're looking for an optimal range, and we can hone in on that with urine or saliva, but the blood ranges are so broad that it's impossible to tell how to work with them. When it's women's health and the intricate pathologies, we really want to see how much E1, E2, E3 [types of estrogen] we're making and how we're metabolizing those... And we don't get that information from blood tests.

Which hormones tend to be most out of whack?
I've seen it go in a lot of ways, but for serious athletes, everything tends to just be really low. So then we work on fortifying the adrenal glands. There are a lot of botanicals I'll use to help regulate the pituitary, and make sure my patients have enough good fats in their diets.

Is it ever wise for someone to try to supplement with botanicals on their own?
I think a lot of people end up in my office after they try to do this! You should absolutely get a professional opinion. You need to find the right fit, the right quality, something that's going to do what it's supposed to. Often the quality in the off-

the-shelf stuff isn't great, or on the flip side, we're making really strong versions of these and they can really change your hormones so you have to be methodical.

What are some natural ways to restore hormonal balance?
You can get started on this part without a professional! We always need the bowels to be functioning perfectly: So eat good fiber, lots of fruits and veggies, clean meat sources, and that will help give you proper fuel as an athlete and for everything else happening in the body. Cleaning up your diet is key. The liver metabolizes hormones and throws them into the gut, and then you're going to eliminate them through a bowel movement. So if you're not going at least once a day, you're going to have difficulty eliminating those hormones, and you'll reabsorb them and they'll still really affect your hormone levels. People always wonder why I want them to change their diet to work on hormones, but you have to—the gut and liver need to be working well.

What about training and activity?
You don't have to stop training. We want to optimize the physiology within the training necessary for an athlete, but it's hard to find that balance for a specific person—Making sure their diet and lifestyle are going smoothly, and making sure what they're running off of for fuel is of good quality. Exercise is an oxidative process, so you need those antioxidants! You also need sleep as an athlete—quality sleep, so you can recover properly.

On that topic, is supplementing with hormones ever helpful?
If we step outside of athletes, yes, it can be helpful. I've seen women with horribly heavy menses, and a couple months of birth control will get us to a playing field where we don't have this bleeding, and they're not fainting at work. Drugs have their use here and there, and in acute care, they can help. But for a long-term strategy, I don't think they work. Birth control does get prescribed often because it's easy to prescribe and it almost always does the trick in terms of regulating a cycle, and doctors don't know about many other options. But there are other options out there!

What about advice for athletes hoping to get pregnant?
I'll sound like a broken record, but track your cycle, and make sure it's regular. If you have been on birth control, it would be a great idea to wait a couple cycles until your hormones have come back to themselves. You're having an artificial cycle on birth control, so give yourself some time to get used to it again. Give

yourself a minimum of four cycles to clean out the pipes!

Do you ever deal with hormone issues in athletic men?
I don't deal with it as often, but I have seen it. It usually comes with poor performance, poor recovery, being sick all the time… It's similar to hormonal imbalance in women. It's usually that testosterone is a bit low. We'd try to make sure everything you need to make testosterone is there: Are you consuming enough selenium, enough zinc? And there are herbs that help supplement the production, but they'll definitely increase levels, so they do need to be monitored. Don't try to do it on your own! It's hard, as an athlete. You train and you know you're capable of so much, so it's really frustrating when things aren't working.

If you had to sum up in just a couple of sentences the best way an athlete can stay in-balance with overall health while still working towards her athletic goals, what would you say?
Big world picture is to be in tune with your body and your health. Don't discredit your own knowledge of your body, and don't turn a blind eye when those warning signs are going off. Just because something is common with athletes, or common with your friends, that doesn't mean that it's right or normal. We can optimize your hormones and make them function the way that they should. Be proactive and be aware of when not to push yourself. You depend a lot on your body, so you need to give yourself high performance fuel to get high performance for yourself. Avoid anything that's going to knock you off your feet or tax your body.

For more on these topics, check out the full conversation with Lia Sonnenburg on The Consummate Athlete Podcast at ConsummateAthlete.com

PREGNANCY AND THE BIKE

In the chapter, we're going to do a quick dive into a question I hear constantly: What should I do about riding while pregnant, and when can I start riding again after giving birth?

Good news for those who are pregnant or are planning to be: In most cases, riding is totally fine.

"People are told to not do anything that might cause abdominal trauma, like horseback riding, motorcycle racing, bike riding... All after about 20 weeks," says gynecologist Kristi Angevine. "But I usually tell people to recognize the risks and act accordingly. Just be mindful of the accident potential, but you can ride."

She adds, "Being athletic through your pregnancy—while staying healthy—is a great idea."

Laura Powers (BPHE, MPT), a physiotherapist focusing on the pelvic floor, notes that a lot of information for exercise in general for pregnant moms comes from the American College of Obstetricians and Gynecologists, and adds a caveat to the 'ride if you want' concept. "You need to have clearance from your family doctor or obstetrician no matter what level of athlete you are, just to make sure you and baby are safe," she says.

That's because sometimes a pregnancy can stress your pelvic floor in a negative way. "If you have stress incontinence—peeing when you jump or run or strength train—or pain, you should be extra cautious and get some guidance if you want o keep exercising, because those are risk factors for damaging your pelvic floor even more," Powers cautions.

Dr. Scotchie, a double-board certified expert in reproductive endocrinology and infertility as well as obstetrics and gynecology, adds her approval to cycling while pregnant, but warns that it won't always feel great. "Often, the hormonal changes in pregnancy can cause fatigue and cause women to feel winded, especially with exertion," she says. "However, once out of the first trimester, many patients can continue to do whatever exercise regimen they did before pregnancy. We encourage exercise with pregnancy, so long as the woman does not develop medical complications of pregnancy for which the doctor may advise decreased activity."

"The pregnant uterus takes blood flow away from your legs. So, your legs won't feel so snappy—it might feel like you're always riding in a headwind or with slightly flat tires," explains Toronto-based registered midwife and cyclist Julie Toole. "So adjust your expectations accordingly. And for any athlete in pregnancy, my general guideline has been it's not about being competitive, it's about staying healthy and mobile. That's a mental shift—you need to realize that blood flow is being diverted... It's not that your legs are out of shape."

No matter what your riding level, as you get bigger, your exercise should become lower intensity. "As a cyclist, you need to consider the risk of falls and the change of balance as your tummy grows," Powers says. "Your center of mass starts changing, so you need to go to lower intensity, less risky exercising. I encourage women to continue strength training, walking, hiking—things like that. And the more fit you are, the better labor you're likely to have."

Toole adds, "The biggest thing is the change in center of gravity and how that affects your balance. And you don't realize it right away. So be aware of that and a bit more cautious. Don't lean into turns as much—you have a basketball in front of you!"

"Not crashing would be the number one piece of advice," Toronto-based chiropractor Carol Ann Weis adds. "A pregnant woman, regardless of what she does, loses her balance because her center of gravity has changed, which means she needs to be careful on the bike to avoid crashing. And the stomach itself might make biking uncomfortable—revisit your bike fitter if it's uncomfortable to ride. Or switch to an indoor spin bike or upright stationary bike to mitigate that discomfort or chance of crashing. Every day is different in pregnancy, so having flexibility in terms of changing your ride settings is important."

"With positioning, I recommend looking at your bike options," says Toole. "The time trial bike is the first to go, but you can extend how long you can ride a road bike by shortening and raising your stem a bit."

"A lot of pregnant women end up getting carpal tunnel, for example—that's because of the compression in the wrists," Weis explains. For cyclists, that can be exacerbated by a lot of pressure on your hands if you're trying to keep some weight off of the saddle, so pay attention to that.

There's no specific date when you should stop training hard. You have to pay attention: "Your body will tell you," Powers says. "You're going to start feeling more heaviness or pressure with higher impact exercising, or you might experience pain. And that doesn't mean you have to stop exercise, but it is an indication that you might need to address an imbalance or back off a bit."

She also adds the caveat that just because your pregnant buddies rode into their final days of pregnancy, that doesn't mean you need to as well. "Don't judge yourself by what you see or compare what you see online or in the media," she says. Do what's right for you.

There are also a few things to keep in mind as you ride into your pregnancy: "Joints and connective tissue soften during pregnancy so you're more likely to get injured, especially towards the end of pregnancy and postpartum," says Toole "Be conscious of that."

"You also have to be cognizant of the hormone relaxin, which increases the laxity around all the joints, including the hips," Weis adds. "Everything gets a bit looser, so you need to be aware of that: things are shifting a bit."

Additionally, Toole adds that yeast infections and general vaginal itching are more common in pregnancy due to increased estrogen and change in metabolism So chamois hygiene becomes even more important!

Ultimately, you need to read your own body: No one can tell you how you're feeling. For a serious cyclist, that can be hard, and giving up some training hours or intensity can feel like giving up altogether. "But it's all about giving people permission to change what they're doing, and that's a hard concept for athletes," says Weis. "If you're a runner, you think, 'I have to run.' But you don't have to run. If it's uncomfortable and it's hurting, try swimming. If biking hurts, try walking. Find another way to be active. You have the ability to change what you're doing."

Reader Question:
Varicose Veins

While pregnant, I've noticed that I'm getting crazy swelled veins around my vulva—is it bad? They seem to get worse when I'm riding.

That's nothing to be freaked out about—but it is something to try to avoid, or at least, to alleviate, from a comfort standpoint! Varicose veins in the vulva—swollen veins that are slightly protruding—are quite common and can get really uncomfortable, especially for cyclists, Toole says. "Blood pools because of the weight of the uterus. They can stick out and get rubbed raw even in day-to-day activities, so the saddle can get problematic. Even without those veins, the risk of engorgement and swelling down there is increased," she adds.

"Compression tights and keeping your legs up as much as possible can help," she explains.

Varicose veins are hard to avoid, but generally aren't truly problematic. "It's really just good or bad luck, and a strong genetic component with pregnancy," Toole explains. So if you're feeling worried that it's caused by your cycling, don't be: You were likely going to have them anyway, but make sure you're taking extra time off to let the swelling go down, and treating your skin with extra-gentle care to minimize chafing.

POST-PREGNANCY AND THE BIKE

The good news and the bad news is that there isn't one set date you can get back on your bike. So that means you might be on the bike starting a week after giving birth, or it could take six months. Midwife Julie Toole says that there's no real reason to wait to get on the bike. "If you feel like you can sit on the bike, go for it!"

"The general guideline for when to start activity again is when the bleeding has stopped, usually around four to six weeks," Toole adds. "Anything internal, like tampons, are not recommended postpartum, so that means you'd be bleeding on your chamois, which is probably not something you want. And early postpartum, everything is more open and will feel raw, to be honest."

"I don't give anyone restrictions," says Gynecologist Kristi Angevine. "Unless you have trauma like tearing, if sitting on your saddle doesn't hurt, you can start anytime. If it hurts, don't do it; if it feels good, do it."

"I think that it's so individual for everyone," says Lia Sonnenburg, a Doctor of Naturopathic Medicine. "I'd say if a woman feels comfortable in her daily activities, riding would be something she could try, for sure. But we'll often find that pregnant women feel a lot of a pain post-birth, even just standing to do the dishes. Once that sensation goes away and you have more stamina, test it out."

Sonnenburg adds, "Riding an indoor trainer at first is a very good idea! You don't need as much abdominal strength then. It's amazing how different you feel after giving birth."

"It depends on fitness coming into it, but also the trauma of the birth," adds Powers. "You can do things to help, but if you have a traumatic birth and push for three hours and then they do a C-section, or you deliver vaginally and have a massive amount of tearing, that's all going to affect your pelvic floor muscles. It's about personal comfort. Especially women who've had stitches or tearing, you probably don't want anything in that area anyway, and definitely not a saddle!"

On the topic of trauma, Angevine adds that a Caesarian delivery might take longer to heal: at least six weeks. "If you're going to ride after a big surgery like that, the risk is that you won't ride the way you normally would, because your abdominal area hurts," she explains. "So give that time to heal." The same applies to stitches.

"Problems after like incontinence or bleeding may impact recovery," adds Weis. "And just energy in general—to take care of yourself and your baby—can vary from person to person. You just have to listen to your body. There's no magic number."

Don't expect riding to feel like pre-pregnancy riding did, at least not right away. Scotchie says that women who are nursing are often not ovulating, meaning estrogen levels can be low, which for some women can cause vaginal dryness and pain with intercourse… And can make the saddle less comfortable.

To combat that, Toole recommends a bit more chamois cream to be comfortable. She also adds that your bike may need some change-ups as well. "Your body has changed and your fat deposits are constantly changing, so your contact points on your saddle are changing," she says. "Be aware of that: The saddle you had for 10 years might not work anymore. Even your bones change: Your pelvis might widen, and again, your bike fit and saddle might need to change. And your weight is changing too. Pregnancy is a hugely abrupt weight gain and loss! So again, things may not fit the same anymore."

"Things are changing down there," Weis adds. "There can be a lot of damage after birth and the differences during pregnancy will likely be more discomfort-oriented." That might mean needing a different saddle with a slightly more padded seat, or a different pair of shorts, or you might just need to stand more on the bike to take the pressure off.

Additionally, Weis says there are a few things postpartum women need to be aware of from a pain and discomfort standpoint. "They tend to have more low-back issues, from the bottom of the ribs to the top of the hips. That's a general rule, and doesn't hold for everyone," she explains. "Because of that, what I like to focus on right after birth is getting your core back. People think it's going to just come back, but even if you're a super dedicated athlete, it doesn't always come right back. So I focus on core and pelvic floor. Two exercises you can do right away are belly breathing and pelvic floor contractions. You can do those basically right after delivery."

And before you start interval training again, Powers recommends starting super-easy. "If you don't have pain in the perineum, start back," she says. "But start easy—stick to flat, short distances as you get back into it, and avoid hills or hard efforts for the first few rides."

In fact, Toole and Sonnenburg both recommend jumping on a stationary bike set-up before you hit the road. "When I had my second baby, I remember putting her in the bouncy seat right next to the trainer and she would fall asleep to the hum of the trainer," Toole recalls. "That was a great thing to do—I was in the house, so when she woke up, I could pick her up and breastfeed! And I could ride as short or long as I wanted to—even if I got 20 minutes in, it was better than nothing. It was such an easy option!"

Coach and Registered Kinesiologist Peter Glassford agrees that taking several weeks to ease into activity—just like you would after a long off-season—makes sense. "Don't push the intensity or volume for the first few weeks, leave lots in the tank each day, and you will lay a great, healthy foundation for your next set of training goals," he adds. "Map out a long-term plan with your doctor, therapists, and coach, so you have confidence in the process and options to allow you to enjoy your first few months as a mother, while getting back to pursuing fitness goals as well."

Whatever you do when it comes to riding again, Weis says, "Don't put time-lines on it."

"Let's look at you going from giving birth to some sort of activity, and once you feel good about that, maybe then you go into a slightly more structured program, like 'today I'm going to run three kilometers,'" she explains. "Then, after you feel good with that, restart your normal training. But everyone is different, from how they feel to their reasons for getting back to training."

Post-ride, be even more careful to do proper after-ride self-care, and Toole suggests that if you are having some pain, consider freezing pads with some witch hazel on them so you can use them after a ride to soothe the area.

But it's not just about if you can sit on a bike. It's about your physical, emotional, and situational readiness. "Physical readiness is simple to understand," Weis says. "Is your body ready? Emotional readiness: Are you emotionally ready to commit to training? You have a ton of hormones flooding the body and you have to re-adapt and discover the new normal. And until you're in the situation, you may not realize the third part, but what is your situational readiness? Do you have a supportive husband or family? Can someone jump in and help with childcare? Do you have a coach that lets you bring your baby along? You have to adapt."

MENOPAUSE AND THE BIKE

Riders nearing menopause, going through menopause, or finished with menopause have one primary problem in common: dryness that causes extreme saddle discomfort.

"A woman's body changes. After menopause, the soft tissue is impacted," says Paula Dyba, the Marketing VP and Creative Director at Terry Bicycles. "A saddle you've been on, shorts you've been wearing—you may find yourself with problems you never had before, and that's from the tissue breakdown that occurs with menopause and that whole lovely process. So at that point, you may want to look at a gel saddle for that tiny bit of added softness without going to a crazy cushioned saddle."

"Some women develop vaginal and vulvar discomfort due to deficient estrogen after menopause," explains hormonal expert Dr. Jessica Scotchie. "It can help to use a more padded seat, and some women may benefit from topical estrogen cream to promote more healthy skin and lubrication production, which can ease vaginal and vulvar discomfort."

Practicing naturopath Lia Sonnenburg adds, "If you're post-menopausal and noticing some dryness, that's not necessarily something you're stuck with. If I was speaking to someone in a consult, I would want to know if her estrogen level was too low, because the tissue down there can atrophy. There are ways to address that, and the fastest and most effective is bio-identical estrogen applied topically to the area. It will improve the tissue in that area."

"If you still want to ride, you have to be cautious," Sonnenburg adds. "Using a good quality chamois cream, and making sure your bike setup is good is key. Make sure you're always really cleaning yourself very well, and cleaning your chamois really well—and never wearing it wet!"

If you're opting for a gel saddle, don't go too cushy. "What I've found is that people associate gel with more comfort and sometimes that's true," says Dyba. "I'll use a gel saddle for a century ride, just for that tiny little additional help for the comfort factor. I think in general, a gel saddle can be really good. But it can also be one of those things with which people think more is better,. You just want the gel in key spots to take that edge off your particularly sensitive spots."

Long-time 66-year-old cyclist—we'll call her Lucille*—who's been through menopause and wanted to continue riding despite her growing discomfort on the bike, explains, "I started to learn about uro-gyno when I realized there were specialists who work with the urinary tract and reproductive organs. People often see one because of bladder issues, often after menopause."

A lot of women opt for surgery, or are told to do more Kegels, she adds. "But athletic women often need a completely different intervention. There are PTs who can do internal work and actually relax the muscles in the vagina [like Laura Powers]. That's what the woman I saw did, and she resolved my bladder problems."

For Lucille, she learned that her soft tissue issues were internal rather than external, and when she started riding a tandem six years ago, it really hurt. "The fit guy started adjusting my bike and that didn't help, the shorts didn't help, nothing helped until I found chamois cream," she recalls.

Post-menopause, she started riding even more, and that's when her situation got dire. "I got a mild abrasion, kept riding, but then it hurt too much to ride. My husband and I were scheduled to go to a tandem rally in the next two weeks, and my regular gynecologist and my uro-gynocologist both squeezed me in. I asked my gynecologist what to do to get on the bike, but she just kept going, 'Oh my God, oh my God,' and she's not prone to histrionics She said I needed to stay off the bike. Then, I went to my uro-gynocologist, and she was shocked too, with how swollen and abraded my skin was," she says.

Since then, she let her skin heal, and started using topical estrogen. "I've learned that using local, topical estrogen is really safe. I'd been doing that anyway, but I was told if you're easily abraded, you can up your usage to two or three times per week to strengthen the skin down there," she explains. Additionally, she says, "My uro-gynocologist suggested using Vaseline and chamois cream—before that I was reapplying chamois cream every 30 minutes, even if it was a short ride. It was really challenging because the chamois cream starts riding up your back…

And it's inconvenient!"

The Vaseline can make you more prone to saddle sores, and lower the longevity of your shorts and saddle, but if your issue is abrasions and chafing versus standard saddle sores, it can be helpful—but it's not the first solution!

Another tip she learned was to treat her lady parts with extreme care: Post-menopausally, you should be dabbing, not wiping. "Wiping can be harsh on that tissue, and you shouldn't do anything harsh to that tissue," she adds. "I've also been told to just rinse the labia, not use a strong soap."

Menopause shouldn't mean the end of your riding, by any stretch. A few tweaks in your kit and your care should make riding as comfortable as it was pre-menopause.

Not her real name.

READER QUESTION:
MENOPAUSE 'ISSUES'

I'm 60, and have had consistent problems with abrasions when I ride several days in a row for a couple of hours. If I wear certain shorts and apply Vaseline and chamois butter initially, then chamois cream every 30 minutes(!), I do okay. Sure would be nice to reduce the frequency of application and/or be sure I can find shorts that will match the effectiveness with ones I have. Any thoughts?

First of all, it's awesome that you're riding so much at 60! I hope I can match your hours when I am your age. But that's a bummer about the bum pain. A few of my initial thoughts:

—How much chamois cream are you using? It might be that you're using a bit too much and it's actually causing you to slide around a bit more. About a quarter size should be all you need.

—On that topic, have you tried skipping the Vaseline? I usually try to steer people away from it, as the petroleum jelly can wreck the anti-microbial properties of the chamois (and be a pain to wash out!). If you don't want to give that protective layer up, I'd maybe even swap to something like Neosporin just to keep things healing nicely.

—Have you gotten a professional bike fit (on the bike you're riding now and in recent history)? It could be that your fit feels OK but could use some minor tweaking to cut down on pressure 'down there.'

—By the same token, have you ever gotten measured for a saddle? Some shops measure your sit bones so you can get a saddle at the right width—if you find the right width, it really helps alleviate the pressure on sensitive tissue since your bones are in better contact with the saddle. (I also love a cutout saddle, personally, and I've played around with a lot of them to find the right one).

—I'd look into switching my chamois. You might like the one you have, but with all your problems, I'm betting you could do better!

—Do you just ride one bike throughout the week? If you can, I'd recommend either switching bikes or even switching saddles throughout the week if all else fails, as a way to help reduce the time spent on specific friction points that each bike has. (Personally, I ride a mountain bike and a road bike in the course of a week, and they have very, very different saddles!)

—Lastly, have you had your hormones tested lately? It may be that you need a bit more estrogen to improve skin elasticity 'down there.'

Maintaining You

This question—about how we as cyclists and as women—should keep the hair 'down there' is fraught with political implications. It's almost always the elephant in the room when I give talks about feminine care and the bike. Often, there are three camps: the natural, let-it-grow camp; the keep-it-trim camp; and the take-it-all-off camp. And while it's tempting to start a hair maintenance battle, the answer is simple: no one is wrong, but not everyone is totally right.

OK, that was actually kind of complicated. Allow me to explain.

Shave, wax, trim, do nothing: All of these options are fine, but each one has a pretty major caveat attached. "There is no particular right way to have your pubic hair. It can be au natural, trimmed with clippers, waxed, permanently removed by laser, or simply shaved," says gynecologist Kristi Angevine. Let's break it down.

SHAVING:

The easiest, cheapest, and fastest hair removal method—but also the one argu-ably most fraught with error. "If you shave, make sure you change your razor frequently. If you notice that you get a lot of bumps after shaving, this is likely folliculitis, which is an infection of the hair follicles. Again, change your blades frequently, but more importantly, pay attention to hygiene. Clean your skin with soap and water before shaving and make sure you keep your razor clean," says Angevine. "For women who develop folliculitis frequently, I often tell them to keep some rubbing alcohol by the shower and quickly disinfect their razors be-fore shaving to kill any bacteria living on them."

Whatever you do, she says, "Do not shave immediately before a ride. There are microabrasions in the skin and it is more prone to infection. Shave 12-24 hours before a ride whenever possible."

WAXING:

"Short answer? Yes. No problem," says gynecologist Esther Yun. "But there are a few things to take into consideration. When you wax, the top few layers of skin cells are also ripped off in the process, making the skin more sensitive and prone to irritation and infection. You may want to give your skin a day or two after a wax to heal over before going for a long grueling ride through mud and rain."

She also adds, "If you choose to wax, you are also more prone to ingrown hairs, so it is important to identify these quickly and apply warm compresses until the hair is above the skin surface and let the skin heal before waxing again. Ingrown hairs can very quickly turn into abscesses if they become infected, and believe me, you don't want to experience this."

Whatever you do, definitely give yourself at least 24 hours off the bike to let your skin recover: Waxing is a painful process!

TRIMMING:

"If you're having a lot of issues with ingrown hairs and folliculitis, you may want to consider scrapping shaving and waxing and simply trimming the hair," says Yun. "A beard/body trimmer can get the hair very short and decrease irritation without causing skin damage. You may not be baby bottom smooth, but you very well may save yourself a lot of grief." But if you do this, make sure to keep the hair squeaky clean post-ride.

NATURAL:

It is not necessary to do any of the above hair removal, of course. You can—as many women do—just keep everything natural. There are a few things to remember though: If you're running into frequent chafing or friction issues, that may be because the chamois cream that you're using isn't actually able to get to the skin. Saddle sores may also be more common, since keeping things dry and clean becomes more challenging. "Hair rubbing up against the skin can also cause irritation and chafing," adds Yun.

Lastly, and least frequently, you may find yourself dealing with some tugging/pulling issues as you switch position on the bike. If any of that sounds familiar, you may want to consider trimming a bit. "A little trimming and maintenance may take care of the problem completely," says Yun.

READER QUESTION:
SHAVING RIGHT

If I do shave down there, how can I avoid ingrown hairs?

In an effort to minimize breaks in the skin, there are a few key steps to safe shaving, and gynecologist Kristi Angevine breaks them down:

1. Use a shaving gel or cream. Apply it and let it sit for a few minutes.

2. Use a sharp, clean razor. Dull razors cause damage to the skin and can predispose you to ingrown hairs and infections.

3. Shave in the direction of hair growth, not against it like we normally do on our legs. Shaving "with the grain" minimizes razor burn and folliculitis (inflammation of the hair follicles).

4, Know what you're in for. Because the skin of these nether regions intimately rub when we pedal, as hair grows back, there can be a sandpaper effect that is profoundly uncomfortable until the hair length is long enough not to poke straight out. This poking, pulling, and rubbing of pointy new hair follicles can really irritate labia and the skin between the buttocks, so be prepared for this if you shave or wax.

MALE-SPECIFIC ISSUES

Hopefully in reading this book, you've already learned a lot about your nether regions and the proper on and off-bike care. But there are still admittedly a few topics that we didn't touch on yet. For this chapter, I turned to Matt Marchal, a board-certified family physician, 23-year veteran of bike racing, and past team physician with Rite Aid Pro Cycling and Team Type 1/Team NovoNordisk cycling.

"One of the first bike teams I worked with, one of the guys developed this terrible saddle sore and I remember treating it in the back of a van during a multi-day race," he recalls, showing his cycling scene cred. "It was one of those moments where I was like, 'Is this what my life has become?'"

My first question to him was a simple one: For the new male cyclist pulling on his first pair of shorts, how should he adjust himself down there? "Fortunately, it's one of those things that you just know," he laughed. "You pull it up and out of the way. Any other way will be immediately painful and you'll quickly adjust. You only make that mistake once. It's never a good idea to sit on your testicles."

The most common issue he sees is numbness, particularly with newer cyclists, Marchal explains. That comes largely from saddle choice. "Men have this strange assumption that because it's a small saddle, it should be uncomfortable. And they're strangely willing to tolerate pain and numbness for quite a while before they learn that it's not supposed to hurt or be numb."

"It's not usually all-out pain, that's not how the wiring down there is," Marchal says. "But if you sit on that nerve, if you're not positioned quite right, numbness is an issue."

To alleviate most of that pain, a proper-fitting saddle can help, as can a proper bike fit. You can get measured for a saddle at most shops now, and you want one that's properly sized for your sit bones. It'll likely be more narrow than most women's saddles, since female sit bones tend to be wider. But that doesn't mean the narrowest option is the one for you, even if you're quite skinny. For numbness, a proper bike fit is a must. "News has gotten out about why being fit on your bike is important and most shops can offer some advice," Marchal says. "I've been cycling forever, and went to med school in the 90s. That was before fitting was a thing. Bike shops just sold you a bike and you figured it out from there. But thanks to word of mouth and so many new saddle options, people are more aware of it than they used to be."

Pain and aches on the bike shouldn't be part of everyday life. It's actually a warning sign, not something to grin and bear. "It's no different than carpal tunnel, where you have too much pressure on that spot from typing too long, and that numbness is your body trying to tell you, 'I'm not really happy at the moment,' and trying to get you to change the behavior," he says. "Depending on your mentality, you may assume that everyone goes numb and it's normal, or you have that 'no pain, no gain' mindset where if you hurt, your workout is better. No! That just means you're going to need a doctor eventually."

It's not that occasional numbness is an issue, he says, but if it's cumulative—happening on most rides or constantly after a certain amount of time—and you keep doing it and don't give that nerve a chance to wake up, you may have a problem. "You can stop using a keyboard if you have carpal tunnel, but it may take months for that nerve to wake up again. Same goes for down there," he adds. And you know what can happen then: the stats on erectile dysfunction for male cyclists may be overblown in the media, but too much numbness and lack of blood flow can take a toll.

If you didn't already read the chapter on saddle sores, go back and read it now! But for a refresher, Marchal says that most guys who've done a lot of riding have had a saddle sore. He's observed that a lot of the time, saddle sores happen for men when the saddle isn't fit perfectly, or if they've been holding one position for too long. "It doesn't start as an infection. You have several layers of skin and the friction starts basically developing a blister," he says. "But that area isn't super clean and you're sitting on it and it can become infected if you ignore it, which guys tend to do. They just don't take time off for it to heal. I have one friend who had bad enough ones that he took his saddle off and did his rides standing, without a saddle."

Don't do that. If you have a saddle sore that's preventing you from riding (with a saddle) for more than a day or two, head to your doctor. Marchal says that his biggest concern with men is that they don't got to the doctor until the minor problem has become major. "For better or worse, most women are used to going to a doctor and showing their nether regions to someone else. And guys are not. But with saddle sores, the earlier you start to treat it, the better," he says.

THE MALE CYCLIST'S FERTILITY AND TESTOSTERONE

"If I went out and tested any road cyclist over the age of 54, they will almost always—if they've been racing hard—have low or close to low testosterone," says Marchal. "And that's the nature of endurance sport. If you start to rest, most of the time it comes back up. Unfortunately, the usual symptoms are so vague: low libido, fatigue, poor recovery—most things you'd hear of with overtraining are the same as symptoms of low testosterone."

The current dilemma, of course, is that supplemental testosterone is banned. "The only way you could get away with it is if you lost your testicles in a farming accident. Any other way isn't legal in racing," Marchal adds. So don't even consider supplementing with testosterone if you're planning on racing. In addition to the obvious issues with drug testing, though, supplementing with testosterone comes with a lot of problems in and of itself: Namely, once you start supplementing, your body will stop making it, even if you're well-rested, or stop the supplementation.

"I don't recommend trying testosterone. Typically, if you start using testosterone in any way, the problem is that your internal production turns off," Marchal explains. "The factory shuts down. So now you become dependent on external testosterone and to come off it, you'll have to go way lower before you get back to where you were."

That's your body telling you that you're asking too much of it, and you need to back off in some area, whether its physical or mental. Even if you're starting to panic that your testosterone is low, it might not be the case: Fatigue, low libido… that could be life, not testosterone, Marchal says.

"There doesn't seem to be an issue for longevity or your health having low testosterone," says Marchal, so low testosterone numbers aren't necessarily a huge red flag. Besides, he says, there's such a wide range of 'normal' that one doctor might say you're low while four others say it's normal. "With testosterone, there's no agreed upon number that's normal. It's usually between 300 and 900 on lab reports, and if I test your testosterone, I don't know if you were a 500 at your peak or a 900. So I don't know where you started, making it impossible to know if your testosterone truly is low for you or not."

Added to that, for the most part, it doesn't seem to make a huge difference in fertility. "If you have a couple who's been trying and trying and trying, you might want to back off the cycling to see if it changes anything," Marchal says. "But if you look at cyclists—from recreational to the pros who are hoisting kids up on the podium with them—you can see that the guys spending the most time on the bike are showing off their kids."

"I would say the data out there hasn't been established to truly say there's a strong correlation between cycling and fertility. If you and your partner are having a hard time, maybe take a couple months off the bike and see, but I don't think it's a problem," he adds. "The more challenging study would be to look to see how many people had kids before they started cycling and then after starting to ride, they couldn't have kids."

THE CYCLIST'S PROSTATE

Good news: "Cyclists, as they get older, tend to be a healthier subset," says Marchal. But sometimes, cycling hard can present as early warning signs for prostate problems, and cause doctors to panic. "I've had patients come in with a PSA (prostate-specific antigen, a protein produced by cells of the prostate gland) that's quite enlarged. And I'll call and ask, how many miles did you ride this weekend, and they'll tell me they did a double century," he says. "I retest after they've taken a few days off and it's back to normal levels. So even just sitting for long amounts of time on the bike can push PSA up, and doctors who don't know cycling send you to a specialist and it goes from there."

"It is rare that I see prostatitis in cyclists. I haven't seen a ton of prostate issues in cyclists in general," he adds.

Because of that, Marchal's best advice for a cyclist is to seek the right medical help. "Try to find a doctor in your area that has a degree of familiarity with what you do," he says. "Find a doc who's also an athlete, who gets what you're trying to ask your body to do. That helps when you come in with a problem: The expectations are centered around continuing to ride."

It's not always going to be easy, finding the solution to cure your discomfort. It's detective work, says Marchal, and it can mean a minor seat adjustment, a change in cleats on your shoes, a new chamois... The list goes on. "Meet more people in your sport and ask around who they use for the best recommendations," he says.

"With a doctor you trust, you'll go in to ask them things and won't try to Mac-Gyver it at home and make things worse," Marchal says. It all comes back to finding someone you can trust with whatever problems you're experiencing, and going to talk to him or her before it's gotten so bad that you've lost a season.

A Few Words on Coaching & Junior Cycling

After all of this, there's one more thing. If you're serious about riding or racing, you may be thinking about hiring a coach, or you may have one already. I debated adding this as a chapter since it's not completely about nether-region-issues, but one common trend I noticed as I talked to women (and increasingly, to men) while writing this was a fear of telling people about their problems and issues. And that really can impact training, especially when it comes to how you're working with a coach and how he or she is creating your training plan.

"It's so valuable to have someone on the outside looking in. And to have an advocate. I think as a coach, my job is to be an advocate for my clients, to always have their wellness in mind," says former pro racer and cycling coach Janel Holcomb.

Coaches of both sexes have trouble talking about these more 'sensitive' topics with clients, and vice versa: Most of the women I've spoken to have trouble communicating with their coaches about their uncomfortable questions and problems that they may be having. And coaches want to be able to help their clients succeed and thrive, but are stymied not knowing how to bring up more sensitive subjects.

"I think it's definitely hard as a male coach to connect with female clients in some ways, and I think that too many coaches think their job begins and ends with a power file," Glassford explains. "We treat female clients like males too often and miss the individuality and really getting to know each client and connecting on a level where personal issues can be discussed and dealt with as a team, rather than having the client dealing with it silently on their own. That might mean talking about monthly cycles, since for some people, it needs to be taken into consideration. It's interesting that something as commonplace and common knowledge as that doesn't get talked about."

He added, "Over the last couple years, as I have gotten to know my female clients more, these issues are discussed much easier and we can just talk about it, decide on next steps, and adjust training as needed."

FINDING A COACH:

It seems obvious, but do your homework. "I'm always surprised at the number of people who just sign up and don't do research or ask questions," Glassford says. "I don't know if coaches are always ready for questions, but they should be. It's within your rights to ask a lot of questions. I think the first thing you should ask is about clients who are similar to you, and ask to talk to them. It's a great opportunity to meet similar people, and the questions you can ask them are the things like 'Do you ever talk to him about your period?'"

He adds, "Coach and athlete should be able to have totally open dialogue about the day, whether that's just about intervals, or it's about having cramps all day, or saddle sores that won't go away, or not sleeping well—things that don't involve the actual workout but that affect everything."

WHEN TO CHANGE:

"If it's just not clicking with your current coach, you may want to look to someone else," Glassford says. That may be hard to do, especially when you're friendly with your coach, but just not working out athletically. Still, it's best to part ways versus making both you and your coach miserable. "That may mean switching to a female coach for some riders, but there are male coaches who can have that commentary too," he adds. "There are men who are very good with communication and/or work specifically with females. Asking your friends who they work with and asking a potential coach to speak to their current clients who are similar to you are good ways to find a good coach for you."

At the end of the day, the buck stops with you in your coaching relationship. A coach can't address a problem if he doesn't know it exists. "Bring it up if it's an issue," Glassford says. "You don't want to have anything you don't talk to your coach about, from intervals feeling weird, to an issue with your period, to needing help with basic skills. It's tough getting to that level of confidence with a coach, but it is worth the investment in time to develop a relationship with someone who can help you achieve goals and work through any problems you may face."

A Word for Juniors and their Parents:

I know that some of the people who wanted this book were parents with young women who were already riding at a high level but struggling with issues like saddle sores. I know that for me, my dad was the parent who was heavily involved in cycling, and there was no way he was going to talk to me about saddle sores, so I wish he'd had a book like this to hand to me!

"Parents are grasping at straws too," says Peter Glassford. "Their girls are changing—and especially when you have single dads, or when it's Dad who rides and Mom doesn't, it can be a tough time all around. I think the end result should just be being comfortable talking about it. A coach may not have the answers, but I think you need to start building that network, whether it's knowing gynecologists or doctors, or coaches you're comfortable talking with about sports."

Like Peter says, you need to create an environment of open communication, where your daughter can come to you with anything—or at the very least, make sure she knows that she can talk to the family doctor about anything. (Or refer to this book!) Puberty is hard, and bike racing isn't going to make it any easier, but it doesn't have to be painful.

Don't wait until she has to bring up these issues either—just let her know that if she does have any problems, you're ready to listen.

If your daughter is part of a team, or you're part of a club, consider asking a local pro to host a night at a bike shop for just the girls, to openly talk about what it means to be female on the bike. I conduct shop nights across the US where we have an open forum for women to chat and ask questions, so keep an eye on SaddleSoreBook.com for those talks!

FINAL WORDS

I love being a female cyclist—especially now that I've been doing it long enough and had enough great advice that it's finally a (mostly) comfortable sport for me! I hope that this book has helped answer a few of your burning questions, and I hope that you'll share some of the advice in here with other women while you're out riding and racing.

You'll notice that throughout this book, I didn't get into any kind of women's advocacy, or insert any strong opinions on some of the hot button issues facing women cyclists today, like if posing for a sexy cyclist calendar makes you an inherently bad person or terrible role model, or if women should get equal pay-outs at the pro level (it doesn't, and they should—if you were wondering where I came down on either of those).

However, the one bit of advocacy I will soapbox for a bit here is the idea of getting more women on bikes worldwide. There are so many great projects and charities that center around women's cycling, and I urge every woman reading this to spend a little time volunteering with some of them, whether that means mentoring a younger female racer, or helping inner city kids get on 'cross bikes (as the Red Zone Junior Development team out of Louisville does). I think any woman in cycling is in such an awesome, unique position of having this ability to influence other women and get them on bikes, and it's so thrilling to me every time I hear about anyone getting on a bike for the first time.

If getting more women riding worldwide just means you take a friend out for her first ride, that's amazing. It doesn't have to be a big project, but anything that gets more women on bikes and riding comfortably and confidently, that's perfect.

There's not much more I can say about your body and the bike that I haven't already covered, but I will say this: I was absolutely shocked at how many people were so excited to hear about this book, and have been excited about it since I first told people I was working on it. From pro women racers, to beginner women, to dads who are struggling with their junior daughters, it was astonishing to me that none of this had been covered before. I tried, and I couldn't find information about a lot of these questions online. That's changed a lot in the last couple years, and I hope that at least a tiny part of that was due to my pushing the subject to the forefront, and great publications like *Bicycling* magazine starting to publish some of this valuable advice.

This wasn't a book that I ever thought I would write. For me, saying vagina in public is one of the more uncomfortable things that I have to do—now imagine trying to publicize a book dedicated to them! I realized though, that if as a racer and cycling advocate and writer, I was uncomfortable bringing these issues up to even my gynecologist, imagine how the average beginner woman feels? I'm relatively outspoken, and fairly comfortable with myself and my body, yet writing this was one of the harder things that I've ever had to do. We live in a society where sex sells, yet we're still so repressed that we can't talk about our reproductive health without getting twitchy. That's why one of the big things I'm pushing for in here is to just communicate with coaches, gynecologists, bike shop employees—just don't be afraid to ask for what you need.

I truly hope that reading this book makes cycling more enjoyable for you—or at least, less painful. I know I learned a lot writing it, and definitely got to use some of the tips from the great gynecologists who helped put this together.

Thanks so much for reading!

MEET THE EXPERTS

This book couldn't have been done without the help of some seriously amazing people. And for those of you wondering about the doctors and coaches listed throughout the book, here are a few of the names that come up again and again.

KRISTI HAWKEN ANGEVINE (MD, FACOG)

Kristi Angevine is a board-certified Ob/Gyn who attended ETSU's Quillen College of Medicine in Johnson City, Tennessee. She completed her residency training in Chattanooga, TN. Her husband sparked her interest in cycling over 10 years ago and she primarily enjoys mountain biking and cyclocross. Given her interest in women's health and biking, she has cultivated a passion for health promotion and counseling patients about the benefits of exercise and healthy eating. Beyond her vocation, she likes spending as much time as she can reading, riding, cooking, and going on family adventures with her husband, Anthony, and their (amazingly cute, sweet, charming) daughter, Roslyn.

PETER GLASSFORD (R.KIN)

Peter Glassford has been an endurance coach for over 12 years with Smart Athlete coaching. He specializes in bike skill development (SmartAthlete.ca) and the optimization of training in the busy lives of the athletes he coaches. As a Registered Kinesiologist, he provides a unique movement-based approach to the health and performance of his clients. In his own athletic pursuits, he is the Canadian Leadville record holder, one of the top elite mountain bikers in Canada, and a lifetime student of movement.

HEIDI BELL GRISSOM

Dr. Bell is a graduate of the Brody School of Medicine, and returned there on the clinical faculty in 2008 after completing residency at UT-Houston/ LBJ Hospital and spending two years in full-time medical mission work in Quiché, Guatemala. She was honored to become the Clinical Clerkship Director for Ob/Gyn in 2010, and has a passion for current innovation and teaching, especially at the medical undergraduate level. Outside of medicine, she is a mother of two, and spends any free time possible enjoying the musical talents of the regional band "Spare Change," which her husband Matt plays with. She is an active participant in APGO (The Association for Professors of Gynecology and Obstetrics), and most of her leadership and teaching training comes from APGO's excellent academic programs, including the APGO Scholars and Leaders Program, which she completed in 2013. She's not an athlete, but loves taking care of patients who are and working with them to meet their unique needs as women!

LIA SONNENBURG

Lia has been working in Collingwood, Ontario since 2010. She began with an externship at StoneTree Naturopathic Clinic and continued caring for patients after she graduated. She is a fully licensed and registered Naturopathic Doctor in the regulated provinces. She found Naturopathic medicine through the stories of immediate family and it resonated with the way she wanted to practice medicine: do no harm, cooperate with nature, find the root cause, treat the individual, and educate. In her spare time, she loves outdoor activities like running and cycling.

BETH LEIBO

A veteran cyclist, Beth began her cycling retail career at Bicycle Sport Shop in Austin, Texas, in 1997. After managing a specialty cycling store [Bike Barn] in Houston, Polar Electro hired Beth as a Tech Rep serving their cycling, running, and fitness retailers in Texas. After a stint in Colorado, in 2013 Beth returned to Austin as District Manager for Texas Running Company, owned by Denver-based Running Specialty Group. Now, Beth works with Assos North America.

JANINA HAAS

Janina has been a sports scientist for the past 28 years, and has worked in the Research & Development department at RTI Sports/Ergon since September 2013. Her focus is ergonomics and product testing there. She earned her Bachelor of Science in Sports Science at Justus-Liebig-University in Giessen/Germany, and her Master of Science in Sports Technology at German Sports University Cologne/Germany, where she wrote her master's thesis: "Sitting discomfort of female road and mountain bike cyclists: Is it possible to optimize the pressure distribution and to raise the sitting comfort by utilizing special constructional features?"

ESTHER YUN

Esther Yun is a practicing obstetrician and gynecologist. She, her husband, and their two akitas spend as much time outdoors as possible. In the last few years, she fell in love with cycling in all forms. Her husband, Dan, ran the Wheelworks Mountain Bike Racing Team, and since her racing debut in 2014, she was totally bitten by the bug. Besides riding together as much as possible, they hope to inspire and help new riders fall in love with cycling as much as they have.

GREAT RESOURCES

Books

Roar by Stacy Sims and Selene Yeager (Rodale, 2016)

The Bicycling Big Book of Cycling for Women: Everything You Need to Know for Whatever, Whenever, and Wherever You Ride by Selene Yeager (Rodale, 2015)

Fuel Your Ride by Molly Hurford (Rodale, 2016)

Our Bodies, Our Bikes by Elly Blue, Katura Reynolds, Emily June Street and April Streeter (Microcosm Publishing, 2015)

Pregnancy to Podium by Susie Mitchell (2014)

Websites

Bicycling.com

SaddleSoreBook.com

SmartAthlete.ca

TakingTheLane.com

ConsummateAthlete.com

REFERENCES

Potter, James J., Julie L. Sauer, Christine L. Weisshaar, Darryl G. Thelen, and Heidi-Lynn Ploeg. "Gender Differences in Bicycle Saddle Pressure Distribution during Seated Cycling." Medicine & Science in Sports & Exercise 40.6 (2008): 1126-134. Web.

Sauer, Julie L., James J. Potter, Christine L. Weisshaar, Heidi-Lynn Ploeg, and Darryl G. Thelen. "Influence of Gender, Power, and Hand Position on Pelvic Motion during Seated Cycling." Medicine & Science in Sports & Exercise 39.12 (2007): 2204-211. Web.

Partin, Sarah N., Kathleen A. Connell, Steven Schrader, Julie Lacombe, Brian Lowe, Anne Sweeney, Susan Reutman, Andrea Wang, Christine Toennis, Arnold Melman, Madgy Mikhail, and Marsha K. Guess. "The Bar Sinister: Does Handlebar Level Damage the Pelvic Floor in Female Cyclists?" The Journal of Sexual Medicine 9.5 (2012): 1367-373. Web.

Guess, Marsha K., Sarah N. Partin, Steven Schrader, Brian Lowe, Julie Lacombe, Susan Reutman, Andrea Wang, Christine Toennis, Arnold Melman, Madgy Mikhail, and Kathleen A. Connell. "Women's Bike Seats: A Pressing Matter for Competitive Female Cyclists." The Journal of Sexual Medicine 8.11 (2011): 3144-153. Web.

Guess, Marsha K., Kathleen Connell, Steven Schrader, Susan Reutman, Andrea Wang, Julie Lacombe, Christine Toennis, Brian Lowe, Arnold Melman, and Magdy Mikhail. "ORIGINAL RESEARCH—WOMEN'S SEXUAL HEALTH: Genital Sensation and Sexual Function in Women Bicyclists and Runners: Are Your Feet Safer than Your Seat?" The Journal of Sexual Medicine 3.6 (2011): 1018-027. Web.

Leibovitch, Ilan, and Yoram Mor. "The Vicious Cycling: Bicycling Related Urogenital Disorders." European Urology 47.3 (2005): 277-87. Web.

"Saddle Op: The Rise Of Vaginal Surgery... For Cyclists." Marie Claire. N.p., n.d. Web. 27 July 2016. http://www.marieclaire.co.uk/blogs/551741/labiaplasty-vaginal-surgery-for-cyclists.html#7jjA2M5yojOJxGlW.99

Brown, Nicola, and Joanna Scurr. "Do Women with Smaller Breasts Perform Better in Long-distance Running?" European Journal of Sport Science (2016): 1-7. Web.

ABOUT THE AUTHOR

Molly Hurford has been racing bikes and writing about them for the past ten years. She first started her career by writing about irritable bowel syndrome and the science of sports bras for *Triathlete Magazine*, and currently writes for *Bicycling Magazine*.

After writing *Mud, Snow and Cyclocross* (Deeds Publishing, 2012), she knew that her next book would be about the topic she cared about as much as cyclocross—women's cycling. Since her mother already came to terms with writing about poop, Molly figured she wouldn't get disinherited if her second book was entirely devoted to nether regions, and so she came out with the original *Saddle, Sore* in 2014. Her third book, *Fuel Your Ride*, came out in 2016, and is about cycling nutrition—a mother-approved topic.

She and her husband Peter Glassford (you'll recognize his name as the coach cited in this book!) also run a podcast called The Consummate Athlete, in which they investigate how to become a great all-around athlete capable of jumping into any sport or adventure.

When not writing about bikes, Molly is typically found riding, running, swimming, or reading. She and Peter spend most of their time on the road, chasing races and good weather.

Follow her occasionally ridiculous adventures at mollyhurford.com, or on Twitter and Instagram @mollyjhurford.

DONE READING? VISIT
SADDLESOREBOOK.COM
FOR MORE TIPS, TRICKS,
AND ANSWERS TO ALL OF
YOUR QUESTIONS.

Made in the USA
Las Vegas, NV
20 September 2022

55683654R00066